The Great
Bird Illustrators
and their Art 1730-1930

The Great
Bird Illustrators
and their Art 1730-1930

Peyton Skipwith

Hamlyn
London · New York · Sydney · Toronto

Acknowledgements

The nucleus of this book was provided by a series of reproductions originally published in the magazine, *Birds*; and the modern nomenclature of the various species illustrated was appended at that time. My thanks are due to Nigel Sitwell for suggesting this project; to the staffs of Westminster Reference Library, the Library of the Victoria and Albert Museum, and the Zoological Library of the Natural History Museum for their unfailing courtesy and help. I would particularly like to thank Angela Jackson from the latter institution, who had to bear the brunt of my requests as well as to contend with the weight of the many folio-size volumes I needed to see. My thanks are also due to Felicity Owen for providing me with accurate information concerning the genealogy of the Havell family, and to Lionel and Maureen Lambourne for reading my draft on John Gould and making useful comments and suggestions. Ian Jackson and Halina Kisiel of Hamlyns, my colleagues at The Fine Art Society, my wife Anne, and my children Selina and Amber, whose often repeated 'Haven't you finished your book yet daddy?' have all, in various ways, helped me to compile and complete this work.

Photographs
Ardea, London 154, 157, 160; Radio Times Hulton Picture Library, London 152; Thorburn Museum, Liskeard 168.
Most of the remaining illustrations were supplied by the British Museum (Natural History), London.
The plates on pages 171, 173 and 175 are reproduced by permission of The Rainbird Publishing Group and Robert Harding Associates.

The publishers have made every attempt to contact the copyright holders of illustrations in this book. In the few instances where they have been unsuccessful they invite the copyright holders to contact them direct.

To Anne

Published by
The Hamlyn Publishing Group Limited
London · New York · Sydney · Toronto
Astronaut House, Feltham, Middlesex, England
Copyright © The Hamlyn Publishing Group Limited 1979

ISBN 0 600 31475 8

Phototypeset by Tradespools Limited, Frome, Somerset
Printed in Italy

Contents

Introduction

Primitive drawings of animals and birds were connected with superstition and magic, and were supposed to act as charms; once the hunter had captured the image it was easier for him to take the animal. Even today in certain parts of the world this belief remains, and taking a photograph is equivalent to placing the 'evil eye' on the subject. In ancient Egypt, the symbolic representation of birds and animals reached a high degree of sophistication, but the element of magic was still strong. With the rise of Christianity, the mystic significance of nature gave way to its use purely as decoration in missals, bestiaries, and books of hours, which have been handed down to us as among the most enduring works of art of the Middle Ages.

Throughout most of the seventeenth century, birds tended to desert the page in favour of the large decorative paintings by artists such as Hondecoeter and Snyders, but by the end of that period there was a new spirit abroad with the burgeoning interest in the natural sciences. Sir Hans Sloane (1660–1753), who was to succeed Sir Isaac Newton (1642–1727) as president of the Royal Society was, both as a scientist and as a patron, one of the most influential figures in the promotion of illustrated books aimed at the dissemination of knowledge. Sloane was very much of his period; a truly European man at the forefront of the scientific explosion. He studied medicine at the universities of Paris and Montpelier before graduating as a Doctor of Medicine from the University of Orange in 1683. His medical work took him to the West Indies when he accompanied the Duke of Albemarle, who had been appointed governor of Jamaica, and on his return to England he brought back a collection of 800 plants. Subsequently, Sloane published a catalogue of the plants of Jamaica and, later still, *A Voyage to the Islands of Madera, Barbadoes, Nieves, St Christopher's, and Jamaica, with the Natural History of the last* (1707–25).

Sloane was a voracious collector and his collections and library were freely available to students and scholars alike, while his patronage was of considerable importance to such bird artists as Mark Catesby and George Edwards (1694–1773). After his death, Sloane's collections passed to the Nation and, at its foundation, were incorporated into the British Museum. In relation to bird artists, the patronage of Sloane was not unique and there were others out of the same mould: William Sherard (1659–1728) and his brother James (1666–1738) who between them were responsible for the founding of the Oxford Herbarium; Sir Francis Child (?1684–1740) the banker, whose menagerie at Osterley was described by William Hayes (1729–99); and the brothers William and John Hunter (1718–83 and 1728–93 respectively). The writings of the eighteenth-century naturalists still have the power to shock us, displaying as they do on the one hand their powers of observation and perception, and on the other their unquestioning acceptance of the current pre-Darwinian theories. These are exemplified by Mark Catesby, who in his *Natural History of Carolina*, was able to write about the world having been 'universally replenished with all the animals from Noah's Ark after the great deluge'.

Science and culture were not solely the prerogative of the rich, although it was obviously easier for the aristocracy and the merchant classes to support their interests both in terms of time and money. By the late eighteenth century Alexander Wilson, the son of a Scottish weaver, had emigrated to America and was fast building up his reputation as 'the father of American ornithology'. The rivalry that developed between himself and Audubon is largely of academic interest today, but it was sufficiently strong for CL Bonaparte to advise Audubon to seek for a publisher in England, where he would find greater interest in his work. The 1820s witnessed not only the publication of the first part of Audubon's *Birds of America*, but also the foundation of the Zoological Society in London's Regent's Park. It is ironical that *Birds of America*, certainly the best known of all the great bird books, was also one of the last works to be illustrated by engravings; Robert Havell the younger, having completed the engraving and hand-colouring of the plates, emigrated to America, while Charles Hullmandel exploiting the newly developed technique of lithography took over as the most important printer in London.

From the publication of Lear's *Illustrations of the family Psittacidae* in 1830–32, one of the earliest books illustrated with hand-coloured lithographs, there is a clearly defined line of descent throughout the remainder of the century; the mantle of the finest bird artist was handed down through the generations, as though it was the badge of office of some hereditary chieftain or the baton in a relay race. Gould worked with Lear, Wolf worked with Gould, Keulemans worked with Wolf, and Thorburn succeeded Keulemans as chief contributor to Lord Lilford's *Coloured Figures of the Birds of the British Islands.* A slight flanking movement through William Swainson, whom Audubon had considered as a possible collaborator for *Ornithological Biography*, taking in Sir William Jardine, editor of *The Naturalists' Library*, encircled the world to embrace Walter Buller, who trained as an ornithologist with Swainson in New Zealand; the two strands came neatly together when Buller commissioned Keulemans to provide the illustrations for his *History of the Birds of New Zealand.*

London, with the Zoological Society and the British Museum, established itself firmly as the centre for ornithological research during the 1830s, although it developed strong links with the main provincial centres in England and Scotland with their thriving philosophical societies, as well as with Leyden, Paris, Philadelphia, and New York. Through collectors and expeditions, information was continually coming into London from every part of the globe. Gould employed his own field-workers in Australia to carry on the work that he and his wife had started there; even for a man of his immense energy there was no way that he could carry out detailed exploration and produce the steady stream of superbly illustrated books that he inspired and published. Missionaries, soldiers, and officials of the East India Company often combined the study of natural history with their more regular occupations; they sent back specimens, drawings, and notes which they either contributed to such publications as the *Transactions* or *Proceedings of the Zoological Society*, or made them available to other authors such as Gould, who were happy to receive them and also to acknowledge their sources. This tradition continued into the twentieth century, with Gregory Macalister Mathews relying on notes from field-workers for details of the lives and habits of those birds he figured in *The Birds of Australia*.

Just as lithography had given way to engraving as the principal medium for illustration, so it was superseded in its turn by various forms of colour printing. Sir Sacheverell Sitwell in *Fine Bird Books, 1700–1900*, describes Richard Bowdler Sharpe's *Monograph of the Paradiseidae* (1891–98) as the last of the great bird books, and from the point of view of the sheer pleasure to be derived from its contemplation he is undoubtedly right. The beauty of hand-colouring can rarely be equalled and almost never excelled by printing. By the turn of the century, when Millais' *Natural History of British Surface-feeding Ducks* was published, chromolithography was used for the most detailed and lavish plates, while the three-colour printing process was used for those of lesser importance. However, it was not only the changeover to more impersonal methods of printing that heralded the demise of the great and fine illustrated bird books, but also the fact that by the end of the nineteenth century there were few new birds left to discover, so the impetus and excitement had flagged. Science and art no longer marched together along that particular route.

The blocks that make up the illustrations to this book were selected by me from those available, which were originally published in *Birds*; through my selection I have tried to illustrate the development of the illustrated bird book – its rise, its flowering, and also its decline. There is one artist, Thomas Bewick (1753–1828), who does not come strictly within the confines of this book, and of whose work no print was available. However, to many people, including myself, he is the supreme English natural history illustrator, whose responses were akin to those of Wordsworth and Thomas Hardy. While for the rest of the work my powers of selection have been limited to those of excision, I am delighted that the publishers have agreed to my suggestion of illustrating Bewick's woodcut *The Skylark* on the title page of this book.

Hampstead, August 1978

Mark Catesby

1683–1749

Slightly more is known about Catesby than about some other ornithological and botanical artists of the eighteenth century, but the circumstances of his early life are obscure. He is reputed to have been born in Norfolk, and, since it is known that he received a small inheritance, it can be assumed that his father was probably a professional man either an official, possibly with the Customs, or maybe a minor merchant. Catesby's interest in botany was obviously developed early in life, since when he moved to London he joined a group of botanists including Thomas Fairchild (1667–1729) who was conducting experiments into hybridization of plants; Fairchild later became one of the founders of the Society of Gardeners set up to protect the interests of nurserymen. Catesby probably used up his legacy in the interest of botanical study and in 1710, having exhausted it, he set off to join his sister in Virginia. He returned to England in 1719 with what was reputed to be the most perfect collection of plants ever brought back. During his life Catesby introduced many American species to England including horse chestnut, acacia, and Virginia aster; Robert Furber's *Twelve Months of Flowers* published in 1730, which is really a very grand nurseryman's catalogue, illustrated the latter flower with the comment that it had been communicated by Mr Catesby 'A very curious gentleman from Virginia'.

The collection that Catesby brought back in 1719 immediately attracted the attention of two influential scientific patrons, Sir Hans Sloane (1660–1753) and Dr William Sherard (1659–1728). Catesby remained in England for a while arranging and naming his specimens, but returned to America in 1722, settling this time in Carolina; Sloane gave him financial assistance and in return received birds, shells, and plants for his museum. At this stage he was still primarily a botanist, his activities as a field-observer and the sketches he made were very much a secondary activity. It is probable that it was Sloane's untiring interest and search for knowledge which inspired Catesby to get more deeply involved in ornithology and to query all hearsay evidence and preconceived ideas; he was also the first naturalist to abandon the use of Indian names and try to establish generic relationships. He developed an ambitious plan to record all the wildlife between the thirtieth and forty-fifth degrees of latitude in America, but this idea had to be scaled down drastically. When he eventually returned to England in 1726 it was to work on a natural history of Carolina; once again he imported many new and scientifically exciting specimens, a number of which he used as material for his proposed publication.

Despite the backing of such people as Sloane and Sherard he had to deal with the entire production of his *Natural History of Carolina, Florida and the Bahama Islands, with Observations on the Soil, Air and Water* himself. For this purpose, he took lessons in etching from Joseph Goupy (1689–1763) a friend of King George I and the most fashionable drawing master of his time, who included Frederick, Prince of Wales among his pupils; he also had consultations with George Edwards, another of Sloane's protégés. Catesby published the first volume of his *Natural History of Carolina* in 1731. The complete work contains 200 hand-coloured etchings and a new map prepared by Catesby of the areas he had explored. Conscious of the interest and novelty of his publication, Catesby packed as much visual information into his plates as possible and despite the fact that they are almost as much diagrams as pictures, he still managed to give a sense of life and animation to the birds and animals he depicted. His contribution to scientific discovery was acknowledged in 1733 when he was elected a Fellow of the Royal Society; some years later he read a paper to that august body *On the Migration of Birds*. Acknowledged as the first real naturalist in America, he followed up the *Natural History of Carolina* with *Hortus Britanno-Americanus, or a Collection of 85 Curious Trees and Shrubs, the production of North America, adapted to the Soil of Great Britain* (circa 1737), and a work on fishes and submarine life resulting from a collection he made while living on the Isle of Providence. Catesby died at his home in Old Street, London on 23 December 1749. The original watercolours for his *Natural History of Carolina* are preserved in the Royal Library at Windsor, while the collection of plants formed by his friend and patron, Dr William Sherard, became the nucleus of the Oxford Herbarium.

Pileated Woodpecker

Dryocopus pileatus

The Pileated, or Larger Red-crested Woodpecker as Catesby called it, is described at length in his *Natural History of Carolina*. It is detailed as to markings, the length of its bill (two inches), and even its weight (nine ounces); the word picture exactly parallels the hand-coloured engraving, which it accompanies. Since only the male bird is depicted, the variations that identify the female of the species are pointed out; basically, the under jaw of the female is black not red, and the forehead is brown rather than red. Catesby was a pioneer in this field and the groundwork he did in Carolina, Florida, and the Bahamas is often referred to by Wilson, Bonaparte, and other later more sophisticated recorders of American ornithology. The *Natural History of Carolina* is very thorough in circumstantial detail; the live oak on which the Woodpecker is depicted is not only described as to height (forty feet) but the differences between trees growing on the edge of the salt marshes and those on the highlands are also pointed out. 'The Acorns are the sweetest of all others; of which the Indians usually lay up store, to thicken their venison-soop (sic), and prepare them other ways. They likewise draw an Oil, very pleasant and wholesom, little inferior to that of Almonds.'

Volume I of this two-volume work is diplomatically dedicated to the Queen 'As these volumes contain an essay towards the natural history of that part of your Majesty's Dominions which is particularly honoured by bearing your august name CAROLINA'. Volume II, which is more concerned with animals and reptiles than birds, is dedicated to the Princess of Wales. In the main introduction Catesby discusses the air, wind, climate, soil, water, and the aborigines and Indians. Those he terms 'aborigines' are the earliest settlers, and he speculates that they may have come from the northern parts of Asia; 'there is a probability that the continent of the north-east part of Asia, may be very near if not contiguous to that of America; or according to the Japanese maps in Sir Hans Sloan's (sic) Museum the passage may be very easy from a chain of islands at no great distance from each other there laid down'. His opinions of the Indians were more mundane; they were people given to war and hunting, they were little, and did not smell, but their womenfolk served instead of pack-horses!

Natural History of Carolina (1731) Volume I, plate 17

Quercus Sempervirens folijs oblongis non sinuatis.

D. Banister.   Live Oak.

Picus maximus cristâ rubra.
The large red crested Woodpecker.

Wood Duck

Aix sponsa

The *Natural History of Carolina* contains several plates of duck; Catesby called this one the Summer Duck, *Anus cristata elegans*, while in the following plate he illustrated another specimen to which he gave the delightfully uncomplicated name of Little Brown Duck. The Little Brown Duck is depicted sitting in the water, while the setting for the Wood Duck is not delineated at all, although in some copies the colourist has put a wash beneath the bird's feet, suggesting either ground or shadow. The actual plate notes are largely restricted to descriptions of the bird, which, while accurate and vivid, are written in the unscientific language of the eighteenth-century amateur. For instance, when Catesby indicates the size of the Summer Duck, he says it is of a mean between the Common Wild Duck and the Teal; in detailing the plumage of this specimen he says 'the breast is of a muddy red, sprinkled over with white spots, like ermin'. With regard to the habits of the Wood Duck, he reports the amazing fact that they nest in holes in trees made by woodpeckers, and have a marked preference for cypresses growing in water! Another interesting feature for him was that while the birds are young and 'unable to fly, the old ones carry them on their backs from their nests into the water; and at the approach of danger, they fix their bills on the backs of the old ones, which fly away with them'.

The tone of this book, with its mixture of readily accepted folklore and first-hand observation, is set by the general introduction to the section dealing with birds: 'In America are very few European landbirds, but of the waterkinds there are many if not most of those found in Europe, besides the great variety of species peculiar to those parts of the world. Admitting the World to have been universally replenished with all animals from Noah's Ark after the great deluge, and that those European birds which are in America found their way thither at first from the Old World, the cause of disparity in number of the land and water kinds, will evidently appear by considering their different structure, and manner of feeding, which enables the water fowl to perform a long voyage with more facility than those of the land'.

Natural History of Carolina (1731), Volume I, plate 97

Eleazer Albin

fl.1713–1759

Albin is one of the most obscure of the eighteenth-century natural history illustrators; nothing is known about the circumstances of his early life, nor is it known when or where he was born. He became a teacher of drawing and watercolour and, on his own admission, was attracted as an artist to natural history subjects by the beautiful colours of birds, flowers, and insects. His first published book was a *Natural History of Insects* which appeared in 1720. Insects continued to fascinate him and in the mid-1730s, sandwiched between his two ornithological works, he published *A Natural History of Spiders* which included a chapter devoted to bird-lice; neither subject would seem to be of popular appeal, and it is a testimony to the power of scientific enquiry, which was abroad in the middle of the eighteenth century, that such a book should be published at all.

Albin's first ornithological work was *A Natural History of British Birds* published in a very small edition, probably less than 100 copies in all, and it set the pattern for all his later books. It consisted of plates engraved by Albin who also coloured them with the help of his daughter Elizabeth. *A Natural History of British Birds* was published in 1731, the same year as Catesby's *Natural History of Carolina*; the title page of his *A Natural History of Birds*, published in 1738, reads 'A Natural History of Birds illustrated with a hundred and one copper plates curiously engraven from the life. Published by the author Eleazer Albin and carefully colour'd by his Daughter and Self from the originals drawn from the live birds'. Compared to the great works of the nineteenth century the description of the plates as being 'curiously engraven' is very accurate; even when compared to Catesby's plates in the *Natural History of Carolina* the delineation is stilted and the colouring arbitrary rather

than careful. The *Natural History of Birds* is dedicated to 'The Right Worshipful Sir Robert Abdy' and, for alphabetic reasons, this Devonshire baronet heads the list of subscribers; eighty-six subscribers are listed in the first volume, mostly consisting of country gentry with a small leavening of aristocrats such as the Duke of Devonshire. However, among these general subscribers are a few of the important and influential patrons of the period such as Sir Hans Sloane and Dr William Sherard, both of whom played key roles in the professional lives of Catesby and George Edwards. By the time the second volume of the *Natural History of Birds* was published the subscription list had swelled to 110 and included a smattering of European scientists such as Albertus Seba of Amsterdam, Dr Stahl of Berlin, and Dr Neuman 'Chymist to the King of Prussia', and for the third and final volume the list had crept up to 122. Albin says in the foreword that he had been encouraged to publish the *Natural History of Birds* by the approbation that had been universally accorded to his *Natural History of Insects* 'amongst the most skilful and curious in Natural Knowledge'.

Within the limitations of his day he was thorough in describing the specimens he drew, but he lacked the imagination necessary to make anything more than a charming factual record. It was the age of the topographer and scientific recorder, and Albin was a figure of his time. He says that he always drew from life, and, in addition to describing the characteristic song and specific differences of the sexes, he took care to 'impose on them the most received and proper names, both English and Latin'. He continues to the effect that 'Only to some of the non-descripts I was forced to impose names, or to take such as the London Bird-Catchers or others call them by'. This reference to London bird-catchers is symptomatic of his amateurish and unsystematic approach to his subject, which is highlighted by the appeal at the end of the foreword in Volume I: 'I shall be very thankful to any Gentleman that will be pleased to send any curious birds (which shall be drawn and graved for the second volume, and their names shall be mentioned as encouragers of the work) to Eleazer Albin near the Dog and Duck in Tottenham Court Road'.

African Grey Parrot

Psittacus erithacus

The Grey Parrot is perched on a disproportionately small broken tree trunk, much in the manner of the birds in George Edwards' watercolours, which would have been known to Albin even though Edwards' own work the *Natural History of Uncommon Birds* was not yet published. Edwards was a protégé of Sir Hans Sloane, president of the College of Physicians, and through his good offices had been appointed librarian of the College; it is known that Catesby consulted him prior to publication of the *Natural History of Carolina*, and it is more than likely that as one of the subscribers to Albin's *Natural History*, Sloane would have ensured that the two naturalists were acquainted. The somewhat comical pose of the bird with its tail in the air picking up a pair of cherries, and the cocky little butterfly sitting on an adjacent stone, owe a lot to some of the delightful details in seventeenth-century Dutch still-life paintings.

Albin's own notes to the plate are simple and uninformative; he mentions that the bird came from the East Indies and is 'of the bigness of a pigeon'. He also says that the tail, which is of a red-vermilion colour, is very short and scarcely reaches beyond the end of the bird's wings; perhaps it was the need to show to the full this one colourful area of plumage that suggested the upside-down posture of the parrot.

The colouring of these very early plates varies considerably; the cherries for example appear as bright red orbs with no hint of yellow lights in some versions of this print, which rather belies Albin's claim that he and his daughter coloured them carefully from the originals.

Natural History of Birds (1738), Volume I, plate 12

CommonTurkey

Meleagris gallopavo

True to his advertisement at the end of the foreword to the first volume of the *Natural History of Birds* the name of the provider of this turkey is duly mentioned; the bird, which Albin calls a Crested Turkey Cock, *Gallopavo cristatus*, was 'in the possession of Henry Cornellyson Esq. beyond Chelmsford in Essex'. For some reason, perhaps the perfection of its plumage, he decided it was of a separate species from the ordinary bird and describes it as being 'of the bigness of the Common Turkies, having a beautiful large white copple on its crown or top of the head'. He also notes that 'the fleshy part of the head and neck was red intermixed with purple and blue as in other Turkies'. Despite the red on the head and neck, Albin attributes to the bird a dislike of that colour, which sounds as though 'Turkies' would make worthy substitutes for bulls in all the old farmyard jokes: 'they have a strange antipathy against red colours, and are exceedingly provoked at the sight of them'.

Albin did not have an enquiring or scientific mind; he readily accepted a considerable amount of folklore and country superstition, which he repeated as though it were proven fact. Details of such straight-forward matters as to size are done by direct comparison with other species rather than by measurement or weight. Despite such shortcomings from a scientific point of view, the plates in the *Natural History of Birds* although stiff and unlifelike display a considerable amount of charm.

Natural History of Birds (1738) Volume II, plate 33

Alexander Wilson

1766–1813

Born in Renfrewshire, Scotland, in the Seed Hills of Paisley, on 6 July 1766, the son of a weaver, Alexander Wilson became apprenticed to a weaver in his turn at the age of thirteen. Although he worked for ten years at the loom, his taciturn character was not suited to this sort of ill-rewarded if regular employment; he nurtured an ambition to become a poet and at the age of twenty-three he threw in his job and took to the life of a peddler, trying to sell his poems along with the rest of his wares. Several of his poems that had been published anonymously were thought to be by Robert Burns, which encouraged him to publish a slim volume of verses in 1790. However, instead of the recognition he sought, he found himself in prison because of his satire on a local mill-owner in *The Shark, or Lang Mills Detected*.

In 1794, along with his nephew, he emigrated to America; they landed at Newcastle, Delaware and then proceeded on foot to Philadelphia. It was during that walk that he shot and preserved a Red-headed Woodpecker, the most exotic bird that he had ever seen, and thus started his study of American ornithology. His first employment in America was at his old trade, but vacancies for weavers in Philadelphia were not plentiful. Since he had read widely and, in pursuit of his poetic ambitions, carried out a course of self-education he decided to try his hand at teaching. In 1802 he took over the school at Gray's Ferry on the Schuykill River just below Philadelphia, where he was fortunate to have as a neighbour the naturalist William Bartram (1739–1823). As before he spent much of his free time walking and observing the birds, but Bartram gave him free access to his library and there he was able to study copies of works by Edwards, Catesby, Latham, and Turton. Reading these various books Wilson immediately realized their shortcomings; even after so short a time in America he could have supplemented them from his own knowledge and observation, and although he still nurtured poetic ambitions he conceived the idea of *American Ornithology*. With this in view he studied drawing and etching, but failed to master the techniques involved in the latter practice, and in due course enlisted the services of Alexander Lawson (1773–1846). Lawson was a fellow Scot, who prepared the plates from Wilson's drawings. In April 1807, Wilson was taken on by the publisher Samuel F Bradford of Philadelphia to act as assistant editor of Abraham Rees's

Cyclopaedia; this enabled him to escape the drudgery of the school curriculum and also to interest Bradford in *American Ornithology*, the first volume of which was published in 1808.

Wilson was tubercular, but had immense stamina and thrived on hard work and frugal living; he liked to make short intense exploratory trips in contrast to the protracted journeys that were to become a feature of Audubon's life. One of the earliest of these was to the Niagara Falls, which he recorded in heroic couplets and published as *The Forresters*. However, from 1808 onwards Wilson was working feverishly to complete *American Ornithology*. Immediately after publication of the first volume he set off on one of his few really long journeys, seeking the 250 subscribers he needed to realize his project; this trek, partly on foot and partly by stagecoach, took him from Portland, Maine to Savannah, Georgia. The following year he visited Florida, and in 1810 went down the Ohio River from Pittsburgh in a small boat. It was on this journey that he had his legendary meeting with Audubon in the latter's store at Henderson, Kentucky, although he never made any reference to the encounter. *American Ornithology* was originally conceived as eleven volumes, but was reduced to nine; seven were actually published at the time of Wilson's death from dysentery on 23 August 1813; the eighth volume was in production; and the ninth was completed by George Ord (1781–1866) who had accompanied Wilson on his last trips. Ord subsequently published two new editions of the work.

In some ways it is a slightly unsatisfactory book from the visual point of view, while the mixtures of birds on each plate are often crowded and bizarre. However, the research, the text, and the conception of the work fully justify Wilson's fame. He was self-taught and could get little useful guidance from the books already published beyond technical names and descriptions. The work covers the eastern part of America from Florida northwards, and his thoroughness was such that despite the fact that there were only ten years from the conception of *American Ornithology* to Wilson's death, few land species were omitted from his record. The scientific detailing of American birds rests firmly on Wilson's work, which rendered obsolete all previous books on the subject and justly established him as the great pioneer ornithologist of America.

Wilson was buried in the graveyard of the Old Swedes Church at Philadelphia. In character he was relentless and unforgiving, he drove others as hard as he drove himself; Ord described him as being 'of the *Genus Irritabile . . .* obstinate in opinion. It ever gave him pleasure to acknowledge error when the conviction resulted from his own judgment alone, but he could not endure to be told of his mistakes'.

Roseate Spoonbill, American Avocet, Ruddy Plover and Semipalmated Sandpiper

Ajaia ajaja (1), *Recurvivostra americana* (2), *Pluvialis dominica* (3), *Ereunetes pusillus* (4)

Wilson's plates were always complex assemblages of different birds; unlike earlier works his notes were full and detailed, with at least a full page devoted to each species depicted. Catesby might have been the first real naturalist in America, but Wilson was conscious of his role as the pioneering ornithologist, and his descriptions justify his position.

The Roseate Spoonbill he depicted was sent to him by the family of his old friend William Dunbar; he never saw one live in its natural habitat, and when he had finished drawing, weighing, and measuring this specimen he gave it to Mr Peale's museum at Philadelphia (see page 30). The Spoonbill encouraged the use of adjectives; Wilson called it 'this stately and elegant bird', while Audubon described it as 'beautiful and singular'. Wilson's first love was poetry and his descriptions of birds and their terrain often take flight as, for example, with the Avocet in this plate of which he says 'This species, from its perpetual clamour and flippancy of tongue, is called, by the inhabitants of Cape May, the Lawyer; the comparison, however, reaches no farther; for our lawyer is simple, timid, and perfectly inoffensive'. The Ruddy Plover is found on the coast of New Jersey, in transit to and from its northern breeding places, during May and October, and Wilson suggests this is a species of Sanderling 'in different dress'. Here, it is accompanied on its migrations by the Semipalmated Sandpiper, one of the smallest of its tribe.

In addition to these descriptions, Wilson gives measurements, weights, migratory, breeding and feeding habits, plus other observable facts.

American Ornithology (Philadelphia, 1808–18) Volume VII, plate 129

Surf Scoter, Buffel-head, Canada Goose, Tufted Duck, Goldeneye and Shoveler

Melanitta perspicillata (1), *Bucephala albeola* (2, male; 3, female), *Branta canadensis* (4), *Aythya fuligula* (5), *Bucephala clangula* (6), *Spatula clypeata* (7)

Volume VIII of *American Ornithology* was edited by Wilson's friend and fellow explorer George Ord, and appeared a year after the great ornithologist's death. Wilson's prose style is unmistakable in many of the notes: of the Surf Duck or Surf Scoter he says 'the facility and skill with which they either glide through the rolling billows, or mount them, excite astonishment', while the Buffel-head he describes as 'this pretty little species, usually known by the name of the *Butter-box* or *Butter-ball*.' However, it was for the long spring journeys of the Canada Goose that he reserved his most fulsome passages – 'It is highly probable that they extend their migrations under the very pole itself, amid the silent desolation of unknown countries, shut out since creation from the prying eye of man by everlasting and insuperable barriers of ice. That such places abound with their suitable food we cannot for a moment doubt; while the absence of their great destroyer man, and the splendours of a perpetual day, may render such regions the most suitable for their purpose'.

Apart from such flowery prose he also gives much precise information about the feeding and migratory habits of the birds, the times of year they appear, and the locations along the coast between the St Lawrence River and Florida where they were to be found. He also informs the reader that Buffel-head is a derivation of 'Buffaloe-headed', and that it is the same species that Catesby identified as the Little Brown Duck, and Thomas Pennant (1726–1798) called the Spirit Duck. Wilson never allows his interests as an ornithologist to interfere with his analysis of the gastronomic value of the different species; of the Shoveler he says 'the excellence of its flesh, which is uniformly juicy, tender and well tasted, is another recommendation to which it is equally entitled', and he mentions that during migration a single Indian can shoot 200 Canada Geese in a day.

American Ornithology (Philadelphia 1808–18) Volume VIII, plate 49

Ramsay Titian Peale

1799–1885

Ramsay Titian Peale was born in Philadelphia on 17 November 1799. He was the youngest son of the portrait painter, naturalist, and American patriot, Charles Wilson Peale (1741–1827), who chose the names of illustrious figures in his own fields of interest for his children. Ramsay Titian Peale was not only named after Scottish and Italian painters but also after his own half-brother who died in the yellow-fever epidemic of 1798. Forenames chosen for his brothers and half-brothers included Rembrandt, Rubens, Raphael, and Franklin. Despite calling his son after two artists, Charles Wilson Peale intended him to join his brother Franklin in the cotton-spinning business, and with this in mind apprenticed him to a manufacturer of spinning machines. However, at the age of seventeen, preferring the study of natural history to that of mechanization, he chose to work in the museum at Philadelphia which his father had founded and of which his brother Rubens was curator. The museum, which was subsequently incorporated as the Philadelphia Museum, owed its foundation to the fact that while Charles Wilson Peale was drawing the bones of a recently discovered mammoth, it was suggested to him that he should allow his gallery to be used as a repository for natural curiosities. As the Dictionary of American Biography puts it 'His interest in the project was thus aroused and he conceived the idea of founding an institution. He wished to make it public rather than private in character and accordingly, when the museum was established it was governed by a Society of Visitors . . . In scope and character it ranked with notable museums of the time'.

As a young man working in this institution, Peale attended lectures in anatomy at the University of Pennsylvania and developed skills in preserving and drawing specimens. In 1818, he joined an expedition to the coast of Georgia and the eastern coast of Florida with William Maclure (1763–1840), Thomas Say (1787–1834), and Alexander Wilson's friend George Ord (1781–1866); the object of this expedition was to study the fauna in those

areas and to collect specimens. The following year he was appointed assistant naturalist and painter to the United States Expedition to the Upper Missouri, under the command of Major Stephen H Long (1784–1864), and made many sketches which were used to illustrate various papers by members of the Expedition. Despite these absences he was promoted on his return to assistant manager of the Philadelphia Museum, but in 1824 he set off once again for Florida. This time it was at the request of Charles Lucien Bonaparte (1803–57), who asked him to collect specimens and make drawings for his projected *American Ornithology*, which was published in four volumes between 1825–33. Thomas Say, 'the father of descriptive entomology in America', a member of the Expedition of 1818, also used Peale to provide illustrations for his three-volume work, *American Entomology* (1824–28).

In 1833, Peale published his own *Lepidoptera Americana* and was elected manager of the Philadelphia Museum. In 1832, he visited the interior of Colombia, and from 1838–42 he was a member of the civil staff of the United States exploring expedition to the South Sea, under Charles Wilkes (1798–1877). It was through Peale's involvement that the Academy of Natural Sciences of Philadelphia was able to acquire its extensive collections of Polynesian ethnographica. Volume VIII of the *Reports of the United States Exploring Expedition 1838–1842* consisted of Peale's *Mammalia and Ornithology*.

Back in Philadelphia once more, he found that the Museum was in serious financial difficulties and, despite the fact that it ranked 'with notable museums of its time', had to be sold, thus severing Peale's connection with it. It is quite possible that a resident Manager would have been more beneficial to the Museum's welfare, rather than one who was held in high esteem but was away exploring for years at a time. Peale moved from Philadelphia to Washington where, from 1848–72, he held the post of examiner to the United States Patent Office. However, after his retirement he returned once more and devoted his remaining years to helping the Academy of Natural Sciences of Philadelphia. By the time he died most of the great bird-books had been published; lithography, which had taken over from etching as the ideal method of illustration, had been superseded in its turn by photography, and few areas of the world remained unexplored. He died at the age of eighty-five on 13 March 1885 in the city of his birth, Philadelphia.

Common Turkey

Meleagris gallopavo

Charles Lucien Bonaparte, the Prince of Canino (1803–57), carried on Alexander Wilson's ornithological work in North America; unlike Wilson he was a scientist and writer not an artist. The full title of this book is *American Ornithology or the Natural History of Birds inhabiting the United States not given by Wilson*. Bonaparte, who was the nephew of the Emperor, was born in Paris and did not go to America until 1822, nine years after Wilson's death; however, as a trained scientist he quickly picked up Wilson's mantle and within two years of settling in Philadelphia was issuing the first part of his own *American Ornithology*. Alexander Lawson, who had engraved most of Wilson's plates, also engraved those of Peale and Alexander Rider who contributed the majority of watercolours to this work. Bonaparte was free with his praise of others and with his acknowledgements; in his notes on the Common Turkey, which run to twenty-six pages, he expresses his gratitude to Audubon who had supplied narrative and notes collected during twenty years 'that he has been engaged in studying ornithology, in the only book free from error and contradiction, the great book of nature'. Audubon also supplied the watercolour of the Great Crow-Blackbird reproduced by Bonaparte.

As a sophisticated and cosmopolitan figure, Bonaparte took a rather grand historical view of the species he described, and was fully conscious of the threat already being posed by the advance of so-called civilization. 'In Canada, and the now densely populated parts of the United States, Wild Turkies were formerly very abundant; but like the Indian and the Buffalo, they have been compelled to yield to the destructive ingenuity of the white settlers, often wantonly exercised, and seek refuge in the remotest parts of the interior. Although they relinquish their native soil with slow and reluctant steps, yet such is the rapidity with which settlements are extended and condensed over the surface of this country, that we may anticipate a day, at no distant period, when the hunter will seek the Wild Turkey in vain.' In anticipation of the extinction of the Turkey and the retreat of the Indian, appended to Bonaparte's notes is a table supplied by a Mr Duponceau with the names given by the different Indian tribes to the bird.

American Ornithology by CL Bonaparte (Philadelphia, 1824–28) Volume I, plate 9

John James Audubon

1785–1851

Audubon is far and away the best known of all the bird illustrators, both for the superb quality of *Birds of America*, his greatest work, and for the very romantic life he led. The *Dictionary of American Biography* pinpoints the problems of this dual reputation when it says that Audubon 'Perhaps the most popular naturalist of America, has so long been a figure of sentiment and idealism, and as a man and as a scientist has suffered so from the touching up of enthusiastic biographers, that it has been difficult to divorce the romance of fiction from that of truth in what was in any case a most colourful and adventurous life'. Audubon's name has entered into the legend of American history along with such figures as Paul Revere and Daniel Boone.

John James Audubon was born on 26 April 1785 in Haiti, the illegitimate son of Jean Audubon and Jeanne Rabin or Rabine, a Creole from San Domingo. Jean Audubon was a Frenchman from Les Sables d'Olonne on the Bay of Biscay, he was a sailor and had spent much of his life in the Caribbean; from 1774 until his capture and imprisonment by the British in 1779 he captained his own ship. After his release he joined De Grasse and Commanded the *Queen Charlotte* before Yorktown; subsequently he commanded several other armed and trading vessels before being engaged by a firm of colonial merchants at Nantes to look after their West Indian trade, which was centred on San Domingo. During these years Jean Audubon lived at Les Cayes and amassed a considerable fortune as merchant, planter, and slave-trader. In 1789, he returned to France and to his wife Anne, taking his two illegitimate children with him; the boy's mother died shortly after he was born, but he had a younger half-sister, Muguet. The children were legalized by act of adoption and on 23 October 1800 at Nantes 'the adoptive son of Jean Audubon . . . and Anne Moynet his wife' was baptized Jean Jacques Fougere Audubon. Once in France the boy was left very much in the care of his step-mother, who rather neglected his regular education allowing him very considerable free-time to develop and pursue his own interests; by the age of fifteen he had already started to make a series of drawings of French birds. At sixteen he was sent to military school for a year, which was followed by a spell in Paris, where he is reputed to have worked for a few months in the studio of J-L David.

During the autumn of 1803 he set sail for America, and early the following year arrived at Mill Grove, a plantation near Philadelphia owned by his father. Here he lived the life of a leisured colonial, but pursued his interest in ornithology and laid the foundations of his knowledge of American birdlife. He became engaged to Lucy Bakewell, the daughter of an English neighbour, and after a quarrel with his father's agent he walked to New York, borrowed the fare from his fiancée's uncle, and returned to France. In France he joined forces with Ferdinand Rozier, the son of one of his father's business associates, and they returned together to America in 1806. Their first venture was to try and revive the lead-mine at Mill Grove, but this was unsuccessful so Audubon sold the family interest, returned to New York, and entered the counting house of Lucy's uncle, Benjamin Bakewell.

Town life did not appeal to Audubon and soon he and Rozier set off once more to seek their fortune, this time in the west; the partners bought a stock of goods in New York and opened a general store in Louisville, Kentucky. Unfortunately, the Embargo Act interfered with the success of this latest enterprise, but it did not prevent Audubon from marrying Lucy and taking her back to Kentucky with him. The general store survived for another two years, giving Audubon time to study the birds of the district before, in 1810, the partners decided to load their stock and possessions onto a flat-boat and move 125 miles down the Ohio River to Henderson. Once again Rozier minded the store while Audubon roamed the countryside, and as before the business did not prosper. It was during this spell of pioneer life on the Ohio, that Audubon struck up a friendship with Daniel Boone and had a chance meeting with Alexander Wilson, the 'Father of American Ornithology' who came into the store. Neither Audubon nor Wilson knew of the other's existance, and out of apparent jealousy Audubon refused to subscribe to Wilson's *American Ornithology*, although later in life he was to seek for each new part as it was published. The meeting led to a lasting feud between the two ornithologists.

After the failure of this second trading enterprise, Rozier and Audubon decided to dissolve the partnership; Audubon then teamed up with his brother-in-law, Thomas Bakewell. Although he and Bakewell were to conceive several ambitious schemes, these were doomed to failure like the earlier enterprises. After the collapse of one of these, a steam and grist mill at Henderson, Audubon was jailed for debt, but was released on a plea of bankruptcy with little more than the clothes he was wearing. He was allowed to keep his bird-drawings, which were presumably deemed to be valueless, and his gun. After this he never attempted to enter any form of business and for the rest of his life lived on what he could earn as a draughtsman and ornithologist, although for a time his children were largely supported out of his wife's earnings as a governess.

Immediately after his release from prison he started drawing portraits at five dollars a time, and moved with his family to Cincinnati, where he became the taxidermist in the newly founded Western Museum. It was at this period that the idea of publishing his bird drawings became a serious project – the example of Wilson's *American Ornithology* was undoubtedly one of the spurs. In October 1820, he set off down the Ohio and Mississippi Rivers on what was to be the first of a series of exploratory expeditions, seeking for and drawing birds, and paying his way with portraits. The family joined him in New Orleans, where he even painted street signs to augment the family income.

In 1824, he returned to Philadelphia in search of a publisher; here he received encouragement from CL Bonaparte, and Thomas Sully gave him instruction in the use of oil paint. It was on this visit that he first came up against the serious opposition of Wilson's friends, and both Bonaparte and Fairman the engraver advised him to seek a publisher in Europe, where he would find wider interest and greater skills. He returned to New Orleans via the Niagara Falls and the Great Lakes before moving with his family to Louisiana. Then, with the drawings he had made and such funds as the family were able to muster, he set sail for Liverpool where he signed up the first subscribers to *Birds of America*. From Liverpool he went to Edinburgh, where he was very well received, was elected a Member of the Royal Society of Edinburgh, met William Home Lizars the well-known engraver who was to produce the first few plates of *Birds of America*, and also Sir Walter Scott who clearly enjoyed making the acquaintance of such a romantic figure from the New World. Putting his lessons with Sully to good use, he earned his keep in Edinburgh by painting and selling oil copies of his bird drawings; the originals were not for sale being needed for the engraver, and they subsequently passed as a group into the collection of the New York Historical Society. In 1827, he moved from Edinburgh to London, but found the English capital a distinctly less-welcoming city; he was not lionized as he had been in the north, nor did people rush to subscribe to his work; however, once the King's name appeared on the list others followed suit.

Birds of America with its spectacular colour plates began appearing in 1827; Lizars produced the first ten plates before he fell out with Audubon and renounced his part in the project. This left the artist in the embarassing position of having subscribers but neither engraver nor publisher for his work. He was fortunate at this juncture to meet the younger Robert Havell, who reworked the plates that Lizars had engraved and then continued with the project, engraving and publishing the entire work of 435 plates, a task which spread over eleven years. During this time Audubon, whose international reputation was increasing rapidly, made several journeys to America seeking both new subscribers and further material, leaving more and more of the interpretation of his drawings to the sensitivity and skill of his engraver. In 1830, he brought his wife over and started to write the text for *Birds of America*, which was to be published separately under the title of *Ornithological Biography*. He thought of enlisting the help of his friend William Swainson on this part of the work, but they could not agree on the division of credit or the method of categorizing the various species, so he turned to MacGillivray instead.

Work on *Ornithological Biography* was interrupted by a long visit to America, during which he explored the coast and palmetto groves of Florida, the dunes and lagoons of coastal Texas, and the wild coast of Labrador. His Labrador journals make stirring reading and are the best contribution to natural history knowledge among his diaries. He also received the accolade of election as a Fellow of the American Academy in 1832. In 1834, he returned to Edinburgh and continued work on *Ornithological Biography*; publication of part-works was a protracted business and it took until 1839 to complete these two major projects, which were quickly followed by *A Synopsis of the Birds of North America*.

The two decades from 1820–40 were the most active and fruitful of Audubon's life; he explored large areas of America, recorded numerous species of birds, conceived and produced *Birds of America* and *Ornithological Biography*, and went back and forth between England and America publicizing his work and drumming up subscribers. This intense activity continued for a couple of years after his return to America, when he produced a miniature edition of his *magnum opus* and started work on *Viviparous Quadrupeds of North America* in collaboration with his friend John Bachman (1790–1874). However, his eyesight started to fail and he only completed about half the plates for the *Quadrupeds*, the remainder being left to his son John; publication of this work was started in 1842 but was not completed until 1854, three years after Audubon's death. In 1841, he bought land on the Hudson River and the following year settled at Minnies's Land, where he spent his last years. After all the activity, he became increasingly apathetic and introverted as his faculties decayed, and he died on 27 January 1851.

Baltimore Oriole

Icterus galbula

This plate exemplifies Audubon's meticulous process of building up his compositions. The original watercolour, which like the rest of the series is in the collection of the New York Historical Society, was begun in Louisiana in 1822. Joseph Mason, Audubon's assistant at the time, painted the dark leaves and the open flowers, while Audubon painted the birds. Three years later, Audubon completed the composition by adding extra foliage and the left-hand flower of the Tulip Tree, as well as the unopened buds. It is a complex study and must have provided a considerable challenge for Audubon's new engraver. This was only the second plate to be completely engraved by Robert Havell, the previous one being that of the single figure of the Bald Eagle, although he had reworked the plates that Lizars had engraved.

Despite the fact that the watercolour was begun in Louisiana, Audubon, in *Ornithological Biography*, writes about the Baltimore Oriole in the forests of Ohio. Always given to fulsome prose he says 'here, amongst the pendulous branches of the lofty Tulip-trees, it moves gracefully up and down, seeking in the expanding leaves and opening blossoms the caterpillar and the green beetle, which generally contribute to its food'. Apart from being impressed by the grace of the bird, he was also deeply interested in both the method of building and the completed form of its nest, which is made out of long strands of a moss known as Spanish Beard. The nest, which is unlined to allow cool air to pass through it, is woven from top to bottom and so secured that 'no tempest can carry it off without breaking the branch to which it is suspended'.

Birds of America (1827–38), Volume I, plate 12

Mockingbird

Mimus polyglottus

Audubon excelled himself with his vivid description of the Mockingbird and its favoured haunts; in his most flowery and poetic manner he says 'it is where Nature seems to have paused, as she passed over the Earth, and opening her stores to have strewed with unsparing hand the diversified seeds from which have sprung all the beautiful and splendid forms which I should in vain attempt to describe, that the Mocking Bird should have fixed its abode, there only that its wondrous song should be heard'. The beautiful and splendid forms that he claimed it would be in vain for him to describe included the Great Magnolia, oranges, bignonias, and vines. A rhetorical question as to the location of this veritable Garden of Eden is quickly answered: 'it is, reader, in Louisiana that these bounties of nature are in the greatest perfection. It is there that you should listen to the love song of the Mocking Bird, as I at this moment do'. Not content with lauding the beauties of the Louisiana landscape and its flora he heaped even greater praise on the Mockingbird itself of which he says 'there is probably no bird in the world that possesses all the musical qualifications of this king of song, who has derived all from Nature's self'.

As with the plate of the Baltimore Oriole, the present composition was built up by degrees; the Rattlesnake was probably drawn at Oakley Plantation in Louisiana in 1821, while the watercolour was not completed until 1825. On publication of the plate Audubon was criticized for producing an inaccurate, if dramatic, study; his detractors claimed that Rattlesnakes neither climbed trees nor had fangs that curved outward at their tips. However, as with all Audubon's studies, the present one was based on long and careful observation and was accurate in all its details.

Birds of America (1827–38), Volume I, plate 21

Carolina Parrot

Psittacus carolinensis

The once abundant Carolina Parrot is now extinct, having been last sighted in 1904. Audubon, in his account of the species in *Ornithological Biography*, gives the reason for its extermination while describing its feeding habits. First, he describes its method of taking the seed of the Cockle-bur, the plant on which he depicted it, 'it alights upon it, plucks the bur from the stem with its bill, takes it from the latter with one foot, in which it turns it over until the joint is properly placed to meet the attacks of the bill, when it bursts open, takes out the fruit, and allows the shell to drop'. Unfortunately, 'the Parrot does not satisfy himself with Cockle-burs, but eats or destroys almost every kind of fruit indiscriminately'.

In an agrarian society, the need to protect crops from the mischief of such birds was obvious, and Audubon recorded that the 'Parakeets are destroyed in great numbers, for whilst busily engaged in plucking off the fruits or tearing the grain from the stacks, the husbandman approaches them with perfect ease, and commits great slaughter among them'. Audubon, being as adept with his gun as with his brush, did not feel obliged to criticize this slaughter and noted 'I have seen several hundreds destroyed in this manner in the course of a few hours, and have procured a basketful of these birds at a few shots, in order to make choice of good specimens for drawing the figures by which this species is represented in the plate now under your consideration'. One of the best of these specimens is that at the top, and on the original watercolour he has noted that 'the upper specimen was shot near Bayou Sarah and appeared so uncommon having fourteen tail feathers all seven sizes so distinct and firmly affixed in fourteen different recepticals that I drew it more to verify one of those astonishing fits of Nature than anything else – it was female'.

Birds of America (1827–38) Volume I, plate 26

Ruby-throated Humming-bird

Archilochus colubris

'Where is the person, I ask you kind reader, who on observing this glittering fragment of the rainbow, would not pause, admire and instantly turn his mind with reverence toward the Almighty Creator . . .' Only Audubon could, or would, begin a description of the Humming-bird thus, but 'glittering fragment of the rainbow' encapsulates this little bird more fully and vividly than any orthodox ornithological description could do. In strictly scientific terms America had better ornithologists in both Wilson and Bonaparte, but Audubon excelled not only in the beauty of his watercolours and the plates Havell produced from them, but also in the word pictures he created, which were based on an enthusiastic and very personal response to nature.

He was a born romantic and a true frontiersman, who witnessed the advance of civilization with confidence and excitement, and no hint of regret at man's spoilation of the countryside or its flora and fauna; he was there to record for all time. 'No sooner has the returning sun again introduced the vernal season, and caused millions of plants to expand their leaves and blossoms to his genial beams, than the little Humming Bird is seen advancing on fairy wings, carefully visiting every opening flower-cup, and, like a curious florist removing from each the injurious insects that otherwise would ere long cause their beauteous petals to droop and decay. Poised in the air, it is observed peeping cautiously, and with sparkling eye, into their innermost recesses, whilst the ethereal motions of its pinions, so rapid and so light, appear to fan and cool the flower, without injuring its fragile texture, and produce a delightful murmuring sound, well adapted for lulling the insects to repose.' Audubon managed to group ten of these beautiful but pugnacious little birds around the branch of a trumpet-flower, and in the original watercolour enhanced the lustrous quality of their plumage with touches of gold paint.

Birds of America (1827–38), Volume I, plate 47

Chuck-wills-widow

Caprimulgus carolinensis

The curiously named Chuck-will's-widow takes its name from the sound of its call; it is a native of Mississippi, the Carolinas, Louisiana, and Florida, where it frequents ravines, pine ridges, and shady swamps. Audubon says of it: 'the Chuck Will's Widow manifests a strong antipathy towards all snakes, however harmless they may be. Although these birds cannot in any way injure the snakes, they alight near them on all occasions, and try to frighten them away, by opening their prodigious mouth, and emitting a strong hissing murmur'. The witnessing of such a moment decided Audubon on the composition of this plate; the watercolour on which it is based was made at Natchez on 7 May 1822, and shows a male bird on the upper branch of a bignonia inspecting a small Harlequin Snake, while his mate is depicted with her prodigious mouth wide open in an effort to frighten the snake.

One unusual feature of the Chuck-will's-widow is that it does not build a nest but lays its eggs on the open ground – 'a little space is carelessly scratched amongst the dead leaves, and in it the eggs, which are elliptical, dull olive, and speckled with brown, are dropped'. However, Audubon recorded that it was very difficult ever to locate these eggs, and if they are found and disturbed the parents will remove them. Despite Audubon's curiosity about how they managed this feat, he clearly never witnessed it since his report was based on the evidence of the negroes of the locality, who told him that the birds used their bills to roll their eggs along the ground; the same procedure would also be adopted if the fledgling chicks were disturbed.

Birds of America (1827–38) Volume I, plate 52

Robert Havell Jnr

1793–1878

The Havells were a large and complex family of artists and engravers and the apportionment of work and credit is still very confused; even the *Dictionary of National Biography* mixes up the generations and the various collateral branches of the family. The elder Robert Havell (1769–1832) was the son of Luke Havell of Reading; he became one of the best-known engravers of his day, and among his most famous productions was *A Series of Picturesque Views of the River Thames* engraved in aquatint from watercolours by his brother, William Havell. In addition to engraving, he was interested in the natural sciences and when he set up his own emporium at 77 Oxford Street, London, he not only had his studio there, but also sold scientific specimens and paraphernalia; he called it the Zoological Gallery. His son, the younger Robert who was born in 1793, also in Reading, worked first of all with his father in Oxford Street, but due to the fact that the Napoleonic wars had virtually ruined the print trade by cutting off the all-important continental market, his father hoped that he would enter a more stable and lucrative profession.

Encouraged to leave his father's establishment the younger Robert went first of all to Monmouthshire on a sketching tour, but returned to London without telling his father and found employment with Messrs P and D Colnaghi, a firm of printsellers and publishers. It was while at Colnaghi's that his work was brought to the attention of Audubon; the timing was fortunate as the American had just parted company with Lizars and was looking for a new engraver. Audubon was impressed with Havell's work and the latter not only reworked the plates that Lizars had already engraved but took on the entire work of producing *Birds of America* (see pages 34–47). The story of the actual way the introduction came about is decidedly bizarre. Audubon approached Robert Havell Senior, who is supposed to have been unaware that his son was working for Colnaghi's; on visiting that firm the elder Havell was shown an unsigned print that displayed the qualities Audubon was seeking, and it was only later that he discovered that the engraving was the work of his own son. The two Roberts worked together on the early part of the production of *Birds of America*, the younger man executing the engraving while the elder looked after the printing. The hand-colouring was also divided with the son colouring the first proof and the father overseeing much of the rest of the work, although the younger Robert apparently passed each plate and added any final touches

that were required. This partnership of father and son was discontinued in 1828 and the elder Robert died four years later. *Birds of America* was issued in parts over a period of eleven years during which 175 complete sets were produced; the work contains 435 hand-coloured illustrations, which means that Havell was largely responsible for the production of over 76 000 prints.

During the early stages, Audubon himself was in England, but as the necessity of finding more material and drumming up subscribers involved him in several protracted trips to America, his son Victor gradually took over the task of supervising distribution. The pressures upon Audubon also meant that a greater responsibility was thrown onto Havell as regards the manner in which he interpreted the watercolours and adapted them for the engraving. The benefits of this collaboration were fairly evenly divided; Audubon had an engraver capable of the finest interpretation, who was at the same time a master of the subtleties of his art, while Havell had as mentor the man who had devised and illustrated the most lavishly ambitious work on ornithology that the world had yet seen. *The Dictionary of American Biography* states that much of the success of *Birds of America* was due to Havell's genius, 'which reproduced both the scientific truth and the artistic charm of Audubon's drawings'. Certainly Havell's judicious use of etching and engraving enabled him to combine the crispness of form with the softness required for accurate interpretation of plumage.

Taking into account the success of *Birds of America*, it is not surprising that Robert Havell should have emulated his master and produced an ornithological work of his own. However, although *A Collection of Birds of Paradise*, has a certain charm, it is stilted in comparison with *Birds of America* and harks back to the earlier rather stiff illustrations from which Audubon had broken away.

The task of engraving and publishing *Birds of America* lasted from 1827–38, and it is extraordinary that Havell conceived and produced his own work while still engaged on the mammoth task he had undertaken for Audubon. The years of working with the American ornithologist not only provided the example for *Birds of Paradise*, but also impressed him with the scope and opportunities offered by the New World. In 1839, shortly after the completion of *Birds of America*, Havell sold up the business in Oxford Street and set sail with his family for America. They stayed first of all with the Audubons and then, after several moves, settled at Sing Sing on the Hudson River. In 1857, he built a house and studio at Tarrytown, still on the Hudson, and spent the remainder of his life there, painting and engraving the scenery of Washington Irving's America. He died on 11 November 1878 and was buried at Sleepy Hollow, from whence Irving had taken the title of one of his most famous books.

Greater Bird of Paradise

Paradisaea apoda

Although he was one of the finest engravers of his day, and the plates that he prepared for Audubon's *Birds of America* are among the best of their type, Havell needed the stimulus of working for an inspiring and demanding master. In comparison to the preceding plates the birds of paradise are stilted and prosaic. However, the birds themselves are very showy and the book can in some ways be considered as a rival to Edward Lear's monograph on parrots which had been published in 1832. Their actual presentation lacks any hint of life, while the static pose harks back to the engraved work of Albin and Edwards and gives no hint that the artist was intimately acquainted with the lifelike and complex illustrations evolved by Audubon.

A Collection of Birds of Paradise is a slim volume containing only twenty-two plates and no text, not even a note of the scale between the actual bird and the illustration. In this respect too, it can be regarded as being modelled on Lear's *Illustrations of the family Psittacidae*, although Lear intended to issue letterpress but never completed the work. The engraving of the plate is, of course, good and the colouring fastidious.

Apart from the beauty of the birds, one of the most appealing features of the book, which unfortunately is lost in reproduction, is the beautiful placing of the engraved plate within the area of the page, allowing a generous margin of paper that gives a feeling of richness to the book as a whole. The title page, framed in a design of feathers from the emerald birds – as Havell termed birds of paradise – is an imaginative and beautiful piece of design. The book was published by Havell from his emporium at 77 Oxford Street, London.

A Collection of Birds of Paradise (c. 1835) plate 3

William Swainson

1789–1855

William Swainson was born in Liverpool on 8 October 1789 of fairly well-to-do parents; his father was collector of customs in that city. At the age of fourteen, Swainson also entered the customs service as a junior clerk in the Liverpool customhouse. Working in a thriving international port imbued the young clerk with a desire to travel, so in 1807 his father procured him a place in the commissariat, and he was despatched to Malta and then to Sicily, which was to be his main base for the next eight years.

His interest in natural history showed itself early and even before he embarked for Malta as a young man of seventeen, he had been asked by the Liverpool Museum to write *Instructions for Collecting and Preserving Subjects of Natural History*. This was privately printed in 1808 and expanded some years later to reappear as the *Naturalist's Guide*. While in Sicily, Swainson studied the avifauna of the island building up a large collection of plants, insects, birds, shells, fish, and drawings of natural history subjects; he also took the opportunity to visit Morea, Naples, and Tuscany and was appointed chief of the commissariat staff at Genoa, giving him the chance to study the natural history of that region. On the conclusion of peace at the end of the Napoleonic wars in 1815 he retired on half-pay as assistant commissary general, and returned to England bringing his collections with him. The following year, he took advantage of his new-found leisure and set off for Brazil as the naturalist attached to Henry Koster's second expedition; a revolution in that country prevented deep penetration by the expeditionary party, but Swainson took the opportunity of collecting bird specimens in the neighbourhood of Olinda, Rio San Francisco, and Rio de Janeiro. He returned to Liverpool in 1818 and wrote an account of this journey, which was published in the *Edinburgh Philosophical Journal*.

At the suggestion of his friend Dr WE Leach, assistant keeper of the Natural History Department at the British Museum, Swainson learnt lithography; until this time such illustrations as he had drawn had been reproduced by engraving. He quickly realized the advantages of lithography, which enabled the artist to draw freehand directly onto the stone, thus obviating the intervention of the professional engraver. After this, Swainson took on the

major task of producing *Zoological Illustration* in which he undertook to meet the expense, draw the illustrations, print the lithographs, and colour them by hand, which, considering that the three volumes published between 1820–30 contained a total of 182 plates, was a mammoth task. A second series with a further 136 plates was produced in the early 1830s.

Up to 1820, Swainson was mainly interested in horticulture and botany; the plants he had brought back from the Aegean went to the herbarium at Liverpool and he was elected to both the Linnaean Society (1816) and the Royal Society (1820); the latter on the recommendation of Sir Joseph Banks (1743–1820). From 1820–25, Swainson lived in London but later moved to Warwick to live with his father-in-law, John Parkes. His own father died in 1826 and, somewhat to his surprise, Swainson received only a very small legacy, which spurred him to adopt authorship as a profession, and therefore from the mid-1820s he was actively involved with many publications. He partly revised Loudon's *Encyclopaedia of Agriculture and Gardening* and then planned a companion volume on zoology; this got amalgamated with Lardner's *Cabinet Cyclopaedia* to which Swainson contributed eleven volumes between 1834–40.

In 1828 he met Audubon, who stayed with him in London and the two ornithologists travelled together to Paris; the idea of some form of collaboration over *Ornithological Biography* was seriously mooted, but it seems the two men quarrelled over the details for such an arrangement. In the absence of working with Audubon, Swainson is perhaps best remembered for his collaboration with Sir William Jardine (1800–74), the famous naturalist, for whose *Naturalist's Library* he contributed two volumes on birds of western Africa and one on flycatchers. Another interesting work for which he supplied the illustrations was *Fauna Boreali – Americana* by Sir John Richardson the surgeon, who had accompanied Sir John Franklin's expedition to the most northerly stretches of America.

In 1840, after fifteen very active years as author, ornithologist, and publisher, Swainson decided to emigrate to New Zealand, where he died on 7 December 1855. His last years in New Zealand were once again largely devoted to horticulture, and on the journey out he took advantage of landing at Rio de Janeiro to collect plants to take to his new home. He is often credited with one further publication, a work on the timber and trees of *Van Diemen's Land and Victoria*, but this was written by a namesake who was the first governor-general; having lost money through publishing in England he was not tempted to get involved again with any form of book production.

Lined Antshrike

Thamnophilus palliatus

In 1816, after retiring from the commissariat general at Genoa, Swainson joined Henry Koster's expedition to Brazil. The initial report on this expedition appeared in the *Edinburgh Philosophical Journal*, but after studying lithography he decided to utilize the collection of birds that he had made while in that country. The small volume entitled *Birds of Brazil and Mexico* is a straight pictorial record without text. It contains seventy-eight plates, of which only the last ten are of Mexican species. Most of the plates contain single birds, with the male preceding the female; the exceptions to this are the very tiny species such as the Manakins, where both the male and female appear on the same plate. The differences between the sexes of the Lined Antshrike are slight and hardly justify a second plate, but obviously its inclusion helped to fill out the book; the only notable difference between the birds depicted on plates 65 and 66 is the fact that in the female there is no distinction between back, collar, and crest and the brown plumage continues along the upperside from head to tail.

Swainson discovered the advantages of lithography in terms of immediacy and drew directly onto the lithographic stone. His work, along with Lear's, is at the watershed between the old techniques of engraving perfected by Havell, and the lithographic masterpieces that illustrate Gould's best books. Swainson worked on a smaller scale than Lear and his volume of *Birds of Brazil and Mexico* is closer in format to a handbook than to the grand library productions favoured by those artists who consciously sought a rich clientele for their expensive folios.

Birds of Brazil and Mexico (1834), plate 65

Edward Lear

1812–88

Edward Lear is best remembered for his books of nonsense and for popularizing the limerick, but he was also a prolific watercolourist, who as a young man earned his livelihood and achieved recognition as an illustrator of birds and animals. Born in the north London suburb of Holloway on 12 May 1812, he was the youngest of the twenty-one children born to Jeremiah and Ann Lear. His childhood was one of outward prosperity but in 1825, his father, a stockbroker, was ruined by a financial crisis brought on by unfortunate speculation, and consigned, like Mr Pickwick, to the debtor's prison. The children suffered, and at the age of fifteen the young and somewhat sickly Edward had to start earning his own living. Initially, he tinted drawings of birds for shops and printsellers, also doing work for various hospitals and medical men – 'I began to draw for bread and cheese about 1827,' he wrote 'but only did uncommon queer shop-sketches – selling them for prices varying from ninepence to four shillings; colouring prints, screens and fans; awhile making morbid disease drawings, for hospitals and certain doctors of physic'. This training suited him well and by the age of eighteen he was already taking pupils of his own.

In 1830, Lear had a lucky break and got permission to work as a draughtsman at the Zoological Society, and the following year moved with his sister, Ann, to lodgings in Albany Street, Regent's Park, in order to be close to his work. His first task was to make a record of the different members of the parrot family and he was encouraged in this task by NA Vigors, John Gould, and Lord Stanley, all of whom were able to supplement the Zoological Society's own collection, part of which was housed in Regent's Park and the remainder in their offices in Bruton Street, Mayfair. *Illustrations of the family Psittacidae* appeared in parts between 1830–32, when Lear abandoned it; however, it represents the first illustrated work of ornithology to be issued on such a scale in England, and immediately attracted much comment and was compared favourably to Audubon's *Birds of America*. Lear's reputation as a natural history draughtsman was made and, although one of the consequences – an invitation to record the animals and birds in the menagerie at Knowsley – was to lead him far from this field, during the next few years before he felt he was straining his eyesight he worked for Dr Gray, Sir William Jardine, John Gould, and William Swainson. However, Lear's contact with the world of ornithological illustration preceded his work on the parrots, as he had already contributed a vignette illustration of a blue and yellow Macaw to *The Gardens of the Zoological Society delineated* of 1830; his first experiments with lithography, a medium he was to use successfully in his books of travel as well as those on natural history subjects, also date from this year.

Lear's work on the parrots was a perfect combination of science and art; he

made drawings in the parrot-house at the Zoo, measured the birds while a keeper held them, and then transferred the drawings in reverse onto the lithographic stone. He carried these stones to the printing workshop of Charles Hullmandel in Great Marlborough Street near Oxford Circus. Hullmandel printed proofs so that Lear could make any alterations he felt to be necessary. and then pulled the entire edition ready for colouring; these prints were taken back to Lear's flat and in October 1831 he wrote to a friend that 'for the last 12 months I have so moved – thought – looked at – and existed among parrots – that should any transmigration take place at my decease I am sure my soul would be uncomfortable in anything but one of the Psittacidae'. The day after the first part of *Illustrations of the family Psittacidae* was published Lear was elected an associate of the Linnaean Society.

The naturalists with whom Lear came into contact over his parrot book were to provide the stimulus for the next few years, until his general health and proneness to epilepsy dictated that he should live in warmer and drier climes; on 31 October 1836 he wrote to Gould 'my eyes are so sadly worse, that no bird under an ostrich shall I soon be able to do'. Lear expressed continual concern about the state of his eyesight, but despite his fears he was able to observe minute details and pursue a highly active life as a landscape artist for a further half-century.

During the years immediately following publication of *Illustrations of the family Psittacidae* he managed to put in a considerable amount of work at Knowsley, producing over 100 studies, some of which were published in 1846 in *Gleanings from the Menagerie and Aviary at Knowsley*, with an accompanying text by his friend Dr JE Gray of the British Museum. He also contributed six plates to TC Eyton's *Monograph of the Anatidae or Duck Tribe* (published 1838), eleven to Captain Beechey's *The Zoology of the Voyage of H.M.S. Beagle*, and helped Selby with the volumes on pigeons (1835) and parrots (1836), both of which formed part of Sir William Jardine's *Naturalist's Library*. The collaboration that was probably to have the most lasting effect was with John Gould, who not only bought the remaining stock of *Illustrations of the family Psittacidae* but emulated the format in his own publications. Lear and Gould travelled together to the continent, visiting Holland, Switzerland, and Germany, while Lear contributed plates to Gould's *Birds of Europe* and *Monograph of the Toucans* and helped with the *Monograph of the Trogonidae*, but by this stage he did not feel able to produce finished plates.

After 1837, for reasons of health, Lear lived mainly in Italy and Corfu. When he felt himself no longer able to cope with the detailed work of bird illustration, he turned his talents to landscape and, in addition to producing a large quantity of drawings and watercolours, published several books of travel and topography covering Italy, Greece, and Albania. He also produced a small number of highly wrought oil paintings, in which he treated landscape with the intensity of the Pre-Raphaelites, in emulation of his mentor William Holman Hunt (1827–1920) – 'Daddy Hunt' as he often referred to him despite the fact that Hunt was fifteen years his junior. This sad and lonely man, whose work has given so much pleasure died at San Remo on 29 January 1888.

Lesser Sulphur-crested Cockatoo

Cacatua sulphurea

Lear started working on his book on the parrot family in 1830; it was an extraordinarily ambitious project for a boy of eighteen, who had had no formal training as artist or ornithologist. Since the age of fifteen he had lived with his elder sister, Ann, who encouraged his talent for drawing, and by the time he started his parrot drawings he was already giving drawing lessons. It is probable that he already knew some of the officials of the Zoological Society before he approached them in June 1830 with a request to be allowed to make drawings from the parrots in Regent's Park and Bruton Street, where some of the birds were being housed.

Lear learnt lithography shortly before commencing his *Illustrations of the family Psittacidae*; this process, which allowed the artist to draw directly onto the lithographic stone, thus obviating possible distortions, had been denied to earlier ornithological artists, who had been obliged to employ professional engravers to prepare their work for publication, or to master the techniques of etching. Apart from the actual printing, which was carried out by Charles Hullmandel, Lear was directly involved with the whole process of preparing and publishing his drawings; he could take trial proofs at any stage and make such alterations as he felt to be necessary.

The Lesser Sulphur-crested Cockatoo is one of the most majestic members of the parrot family, and it was, not surprisingly, some of the brighter species which attracted most attention. William Swainson was particularly delighted with two plates and wrote to Lear 'I received yesterday, with great pleasure the numbers of your beautiful work. To repeat my recorded opinion of it, as a whole, is unnecessary but there are two plates which more especially deserve the highest praise; they are the New Holland Palaeornis, and the red and yellow Macaw. The latter is in my estimation equal to any figure ever painted by Barraband or Audubon, for grace of design, perspective, or anatomical accuracy. I am so particularly pleased with these, that I should feel much gratified by possessing a duplicate copy of each. They will then be framed, as fit companions in my drawing-room to hang by the side of a pair by my friend Audubon'. High praise indeed for so young a man. Swainson's suggestion of framing has, unfortunately, been followed all too often, and out of the 175 sets issued by Lear many are now either broken up or incomplete due to such depredations.

Illustrations of the family Psittacidae (1830–32), plate 4

Budgerigar

Melopsittacus undulatus

The Budgerigar is the smallest member of the parrot family, and in Lear's monograph is placed directly after the Macaws, which gives added emphasis to its smallness in relation to its congeners, despite the fact that the preceding plate depicts the so-called Dwarf Parakeet Macaw. Lear called the specimen he figured the Undulated Parrakeet, *Nanodes undulatus*. Although the Budgerigar had been described scientifically as early as the 1790s, a mere twenty years after Captain Cook first landed in Australia, it was not until 1831 that a stuffed specimen was shown at the Linnaean Society in London, where it created a sensation. This specimen was presumably the actual one that Lear drew, as the presentation and the preparation of the plate coincide so precisely in date. There is a stiffness about Lear's Budgerigar in comparison to the other plates in his monograph, which also emphasizes the fact that it was not drawn from life.

The first live Budgerigar to reach England was brought back by the Goulds from Australia in 1840 (see note on page 90). Once the species was introduced live into Europe it proved to be an ideal cage-bird, since due to the severity of conditions in its natural habitat, it is forced to breed prolifically and at an early age in order to survive. The dry lands of Australia are hardly a congenial breeding ground, and any species intent on survival must be able to take losses and make the best of any situation.

Illustrations of the family Psittacidae (1830–32), plate 13

Crimson-winged Parakeet

Aprosmictus erythropterus

Plates 14 and 15 of the *Illustrations of the family Psittacidae* were devoted by Lear to the beautiful Crimson-winged Parakeet – or Parrakeet as he always spelled it – in order to show both the difference between the sexes and the difference between the young and the mature male bird. In contrast to the fully grown cock, the hen is more uniformly green with only the edges of its wings displaying the crimson plumage, which gives the bird its name. The inclusion of the second plate also gave Lear the opportunity to show the younger male from the rear with its tail fanned out in order to give the full spread of its feathers.

Regrettably, there is no letterpress to *Illustrations of the family Psittacidae*; Lear had originally intended to issue the work in fourteen parts, but he abandoned the project after publication of the twelfth folio. Writing to Sir William Jardine he said 'neither will there be (from me) any letterpress. Their one publication was a speculation which so far as it made me known procured me employment, but in the matter of money occasionally caused loss'. Having suffered terribly the humiliation of his father's bankruptcy, Lear was punctilious in the prompt payment of his debts, but a number of his well-to-do subscribers were more dilatory in settling accounts, with the result that Lear and his sister often went short.

Despite the fact that the work was never completed, *Illustrations of the family Psittacidae* with its folio-size plates, lithographic outline, and careful colouring pioneered the format that was to be rapidly developed by Gould, and set the pattern that was to be adopted almost universally until the technology of photographic reproduction rendered the hand-coloured plate obsolete. Lear obviously intended to write detailed notes on the appearance of each bird; with the help of a keeper he took measurements of the beak, the legs, and even the wingspan, which with some of the bigger members of the parrot family must have presented quite a problem.

Illustrations of the family Psittacidae (1830–32), plate 15

Kuhl's Ruffed Lory

Vini kuhlii

When Lear started working on the parrot family he and Ann were living in a small top-floor flat at 28 Upper North Place off Gray's Inn Road, where Lear coloured the plates that Hullmandel had printed. Gradually the plates took over much of the flat, and he wrote to a friend suggesting that if he visited them at Upper North Place he might have to sit in the grate 'seeing, that of the six chairs I possess 5 are at present occupied with lithographic prints – the whole of my exalted and delightful tenement in fact overflows with them'. Despite his claim that he sometimes incurred losses on the publication, he moved to 61 Albany Street, Regent's Park, in order to be nearer to the Zoo, and it was from this address that the last parts of *Illustrations of the family Psittacidae* were issued.

For a few years, from 1830 to the time he went to Knowsley to work for Lord Derby, all his commissions centred on the Zoological Society, and the convenience of his new lodgings must have greatly facilitated his work. He contributed illustrations to the *Transactions of the Zoological Society*, *The Zoology of the Voyage of H.M.S. Beagle*, and for a volume on *Tortoises Terrapins and Turtles*, although the latter was not published until 1872. He had quickly gained the respect of ornithologists and others interested in the natural sciences, as is shown by the subscription list to *Illustrations of the family Psittacidae* which, in addition to Lord Stanley – son of the Earl of Derby – included most of the eminent naturalists of the day such as Vigors, Jardine, Bonaparte, Gould, and Selby.

Illustrations of the family Psittacidae (1830–32), plate 38

Eagle Owl

Bubo bubo

Although the majority of plates in *Birds of Europe* were lithographed by Elizabeth Gould after her husband's drawings, Edward Lear contributed a number of plates, which he not only drew but transferred to the stone himself; as with the plates for his own work on the parrot family the printing was done by Charles Hullmandel. The Great-horned Owl, or Eagle Owl, which is the subject of this plate, is the largest European owl. Its main habitat is in the desolate regions of Norway, Sweden. and Russia, although its actual geographic spread is immense; according to Gould's notes it is diffused throughout China and is occasionally found as far away as the Cape of Good Hope.

Like all owls, and true to its name, the Eagle Owl is a predator. Gould waxes lyrical on the subject of this magnificent bird and the way in which it falls upon its prey – 'Perched upon some branch, and obscured by the shadows of evening, it marks its ill-fated quarry; the fawn reposing among the fern, – the hare nibbling the grass, – the grouse couching among the heath; – silently and rapidly down it pounces, strikes its talons into its victim, and commences the work of destruction. Less noble game, such as moles, rats and lizards, may also be ranked among its articles of food'. The female does not appear in the book, but Gould notes that she is slightly larger than her mate and slightly brighter in colouring; as to scale, the bird depicted by Lear is three-quarters life-size.

Having only visited Holland, Germany, and Switzerland with Gould, Lear had presumably not seen the Eagle Owl in its wild state; the specimen depicted was supplied by the Hon. Daniel Finch, son of the Earl of Aylesford.

Birds of Europe, by John Gould (1832–37), Volume I, plate 37

E. Lear. del.

Whistling Swan

Cygnus cygnus

The Whistling Swan is one of the most beautiful and best-known plates that Lear produced for Gould's *Birds of Europe*. The immense bird, drawn one-third life-size, fills most of the plate but thanks to Lear's art does not crowd it; by placing the bird at the water's edge Lear has been able, in a natural and lifelike manner, to depict the Whistling Swan standing, but with its neck arched in an elegant curve bringing the bird's face and beak down towards the water, as if in search of food. This posture enabled Lear to depict the bird to advantage and on as large a scale as the folio-size plate would allow. Due to the immense power of the swan and its ability to fly very long distances, it is known in many parts of the northern hemisphere; in summer it congregates within the Arctic Circle, but in winter migrates southwards to northern parts of Europe and Asia, although the Whistling Swan is more often regarded as a native of North America and Canada. Like the Canada Goose (see page 28) described by Wilson, it can therefore be regarded as a native of the Polar regions, whose winter migrations take it to many parts of the globe. The swans normally migrate in twos and threes, but during very severe winters fairly large flocks can be seen. According to Gould 'its usual call-note resembles the sound of the word *hoop*, loudly and harshly uttered several times in succession'.

It is interesting to note that nearly all the birds that Lear drew and lithographed for Gould were of the larger European species; this possibly has something to do with his seemingly unfounded obsession regarding the state of his eyesight.

Birds of Europe by John Gould (1832–37), Volume V, plate 355

Great Auk

Pinguinis impennis

The Great Auk has always been regarded as something of an oddity, a romantic yet slightly absurd bird. Birds that are unable to fly are traditional butts for jokers and rhymesters; the vestigial wing of the Great Auk acted as an oar as it paddled its solitary course in the frozen seas of the far north. 'The seas of the polar region, agitated with storms and covered with immense icebergs, form the congenial habitat of the Great Auk: here it may be said to pass the whole of its existence, braving the severest winters with the utmost impunity, so that it is only occasionally seen, and that at distant intervals, even so far south as the seas adjacent to the northernmost parts of the British Islands.' The very remoteness of this strange bird immediately imbued it with a touch of romance, bordering on the fairy tale.

Gould's success as a businessman created a considerable amount of envy, and he has often been accused of exploiting other artists' work without proper acknowledgement or reward; it is plates such as this one of the Great Auk, which have fuelled such accusations, for, although it is quite clearly signed by Edward Lear in the plate, the subscript reads 'Drawn from Nature and on the stone by J & E Gould. Printed by C Hullmandel'. It is a weakness of human nature to attribute the worst motives to people who reach the top, while lesser mortals are allowed the occasional slip; it is actually far more likely that the credit lines were inserted by Hullmandel rather than Gould, and such mistakes and oversights are no more than printer's errors; but regrettable nonetheless. The fact that Lear oversaw much of the printing of *Birds of Europe*, would also tend to exonerate the author from such charges. Although they worked together quite a lot, Lear did not particularly like Gould, describing him as a harsh and violent man despite a certain jollity and bonhomie; 'At the Zoological Society at 33 Bruton Street, at Hullmandel's – at Broad Street ever the same, perservering hard working toiler in his own line, – but ever as unfeeling for those about him'.

Birds of Europe by John Gould (1832–37) Volume V, plate 400

Dalmatian Pelican

Pelecanus crispus

As with the Whistling Swan and the Great Auk, Lear is again tackling one of the larger species of European birds. Plates 405 and 406 of this magnificent five-volume work are both by Lear and both devoted to pelicans; the former to the White Pelican, *Pelecanus onocrotalus*, whose chief difference from the present species is the absence of the 'beautiful crest or mane of narrow, elongated, silky feathers'. The subtlety of this differential probably accounted for the fact that the Dalmatian Pelican was not identified as a separate species until the 1820s. In his note Gould wrote 'A bird of such striking magnitude as the present having so long escaped observation even on the shores of Europe, what may we not expect from those more distant countries to which the scrutinising eye of the naturalist has seldom penetrated? Although this species has been introduced to the notice of the scientific within the last few years only, it has doubtless long abounded where it is now found'.

The specimen depicted was sent to John Gould by Baron de Feldegg, and was one of twenty-four birds killed by him on the shores of Dalmatia. In the Baron's letter, which accompanied the specimen, he said 'The first example of this bird that came under my notice was shot by myself in the year 1828 in Dalmatia, and was sent to the Imperial Cabinet in Vienna. Two years after this, Messrs Rüppell and Kittlitz met with this species in Abyssinia, where, however, it would appear to be very scarce, as those gentlemen procured only a single specimen'. De Feldegg went on to describe the Dalmatian Pelican as very cunning and extremely difficult to shoot, although he had witnessed it coming through Bosnia, Yugoslavia, in flocks of up to a dozen at a time.

Birds of Europe by John Gould (1832–37), Volume V, plate 406

Crested Guan

Penelope purpurascens

Lord Stanley, later the thirteenth Earl of Derby, came across Lear while he was
working on *Illustrations of the family Psittacidae* and subscribed to that work.
As soon as Lear was finished with his parrots he was invited to stay at
Knowsley, Lord Derby's seat in Lancashire, to draw some of the birds and
animals in the menagerie. Lord Derby's private menagerie was legendary, and
Josef Wolf, who went to Knowsley in 1850, wrote 'Whatever the most
lavish expenditure, the influence of the head of a great house, untiring foreign
collectors and correspondents, extravagant enthusiasm, and dogged pertinacity
could do to enrich the collections, living and dead, had been done. There was,
perhaps, nothing to equal them at that time, and I suppose that, in many
respects, they have not been surpassed'. Lear went there strictly as an employee,
and it is quite possible that Lord Derby would have remained virtually
unaware of his presence if it had not been for his grandchildren, who delighted
in the artist's sense of fun. The books of nonsense owe their origins to Lear's
visit to Knowsley, and because the children found him such amusing company
the family got to know him well, with the result that throughout his life four
generations of the Stanley family were pleased to act as both friend and patron.
Lear spent a lot of time between 1832–37 at Knowsley, and at times found it
very stifling 'The uniform apathetic tone assumed by lofty society irks me
dreadfully' he wrote, 'nothing I long for half so much as to giggle heartily and
to hop on one leg down the great gallery – but I dare not'.

 The Gleanings, which was privately published in 1846, is not solely devoted
to ornithological subjects, but includes a puma, turtles, marmots, and a Javan
Squirrel among many others. The text and notes were written by Dr JE Gray
(1785–1840) of the British Museum who, in the very formal introduction, says
'The following plates are selected from the series of drawings made by
Mr Edward Lear from the living animals in the Right Honourable the Earl of
Derby's Menagerie at Knowsley Hall, forming part of the large collections of
Zoological drawings in his Lordship's library. They were lithographed with
great care by Mr J.W. Moore, and coloured by Mr Bayfield. Their chief value
consists in their being accurate representations of living specimens'. Unlike the
Illustrations of the family Psittacidae, for *The Gleanings* Lear only made the
watercolours, the rest of the work being carried out by others.

The Gleanings from the Menagerie at Knowsley Hall (1846), plate 11

John Gould

1804–81

Second only in importance to Audubon as a bird illustrator is John Gould, although it is hard to imagine a starker contrast to Audubon's romantic childhood than Gould's very English background. Born at Lyme Regis in Dorset on 14 September 1804, the son of a gardener, he moved to Windsor in 1818 when his father was appointed foreman gardener at the Castle. He received his training from JT Aiton the head gardener, and one of his tasks as a fourteen-year-old boy was to pick the dandelions for Queen Charlotte's favourite tea. In addition to plants, Gould studied the birds at Windsor and made his first attempts at taxidermy; later he went to Yorkshire as gardener to Sir William Ingleby at Ripley Castle. In 1827, he came south again this time to London, having obtained the post of taxidermist to the newly formed Zoological Society where, among other tasks, he had to stuff the first giraffe ever brought to England, which had been given to King George IV; the animal, painted by JL Agasse and charicatured by William Heath, had entered into the romantic soul of the English. This craving for exoticism, coupled with a scientific desire for knowledge, stimulated the demand for colour-plate bird books, especially those that depicted rare and colourful species.

If the giraffe was Gould's biggest single task, the collection of bird skins from the Himalayas brought to the Zoological Society in 1830 represented the most important stimulus to his talents. The collection was the first of its kind to arrive in England; Gould himself was still unskilled as an ornithologist, so the work of identification was undertaken by his friend and mentor Nicholas Aylward Vigors, the first secretary of the Zoological Society. The possibilities offered by the collection, from the point of view of publication were immediately seized upon by Gould, who had recently married Elizabeth Coxen, a very skilful draughtswoman; she was the daughter of a Kentish sea-captain and had trained as a governess. Elizabeth Gould quickly mastered the art of lithography, and from their marriage until her early death at the age of thirty-seven in 1841, undertook the transfer of most of her husband's drawings to the lithographic stone. Gould's is an extraordinary success story for, although his talents as a draughtsman were restricted to rough but vigorous sketches, he had great flair for organizing others which, coupled with his own enthusiasm and powers of concentration, enabled him to produce some of the greatest bird books of all time.

The first scientific results from the Himalayan collection were published by Vigors in the *Proceedings of the Zoological Society*, but Gould could see the potential market for illustrations of these exotic birds, and when he failed to find a publisher, decided to undertake the work himself. He made preliminary drawings which his wife, Elizabeth, then worked up and lithographed; these were then printed by Charles Hullmandel, who had already demonstrated his skill with the printing of Lear's book on parrots. The scientific descriptions and text for the book were prepared by Vigors, who took the opportunity of naming a previously unrecorded species of Sunbird *Aethyopyga gouldiae* in honour of Elizabeth Gould; in addition to using Hullmandel, Gould also adopted the Lear format of folio-size plates, which were issued in monthly parts during 1831–32, under the title of *A Century of Birds hitherto unfigured, from the Himalayan Mountains* (see page 80). Lear is reputed to have helped Mrs Gould with some of the foregrounds in *A Century of Birds*, but this is unsubstantiated. However, he did assist the Goulds with their next three publications, contributing completed plates for *Birds of Europe* (see pages 66–72) and *A Monograph of the Ramphastidae or family of Toucans* and help with *A Monograph of the Trogonidae or family of Trogons*, that was not published until 1838 when Lear felt his sight had deteriorated to such an extent that he could no longer cope with the detailed work.

Gould had made a considerable breakthrough with these four works; *The Dictionary of National Biography* describes *A Century of Birds* as 'by far the most accurately illustrated work on foreign ornithology that had been issued up to that period', while of the thirty-four species of Trogons covered in the monograph devoted to that genus a dozen were previously unrecorded. In addition to the scientific importance of these works, Gould had hit on and perfected the system which he was to pursue throughout his life, and which was to earn him a considerable fortune. He collected and set up the specimens, making rough sketches, which he annotated copiously, so that the various artists he employed could work them up into detailed watercolours ready for transfer to the lithographic stone. Initially, this work was done by Elizabeth Gould, but after her death was most frequently carried out either by William Hart or Henry Constantine Richter (1821–1902). Gould then saw the work through the press and into the hands of his subscribers. If his reputation had to stand on these works alone he would still be regarded as an important figure among ornithological illustrators, but his major work was still to come.

After his work on Darwin's *Zoology of the Voyage of H.M.S. Beagle* (1832–36) (see page 86), Gould's attention was drawn by some specimens sent home by Charles and Stephen Coxen, his wife's brothers, who had emigrated to New South Wales. Most of these species were unrecorded and much of the

Australian subcontinent was still unexplored. Using the specimens supplied by the Coxen brothers Gould started issuing his *Synopsis of the Birds of Australia*, which appeared in parts between 1837–38; this work showed the heads of 168 species fitted into seventy-three lithographic plates. The thirst for scientific discovery ensured the success of the *Synopsis of the Birds of Australia*, and Gould decided that he should go to Australia himself to organize the systematic collecting of specimens. Along with this wife and an assistant zoologist, John Gilbert, he embarked for Australia in May 1838; they landed in Tasmania and, leaving Elizabeth in Hobart, Gould set out to explore. The following year they moved to Yarrundi in New South Wales to stay with the Coxens. While Gilbert was despatched on an expedition of exploration to Western Australia, Gould himself used the time to explore both New South Wales and to make his way down into South Australia. The Goulds returned to England during 1840 and immediately started issuing *Birds of Australia*, the first part of which appeared in December that year, just three months after their arrival in London.

Gould and Gilbert were able to add several hundred new species to those already known to inhabit Australia, through their thorough methods of collecting, and they shipped back to England several thousand specimens of birds, plants, nests, and so on. Never missing an opportunity, Gould secured royal patronage for *Birds of Australia* and permission to dedicate the work to Queen Victoria; in gratitude he named new species after both the Queen and her Consort – the Victoria Riflebird and Prince Albert's Lyrebird. Less than a year after their return from Australia Elizabeth Gould died, leaving her husband with a young family and without the support and enthusiasm of his most devoted and able lithographer; up to that time she and Lear had been the only lithographers who had met Gould's exacting standards. Subscribers were waiting impatiently for further parts of *Birds of Australia*; specimens were still coming in from the Coxens, Gilbert, and other field assistants whom Gould had taken on, and he was not able to produce his own lithographs. Nothing is known about the early life and training of Henry Ritcher, who, as a young man of twenty-one, stepped in and lithographed all the outstanding parts of *Birds of Australia*, and continued to work for Gould as one of his two regular lithographic artists until the latter's death in 1881.

John Gilbert, who had returned to England for a short spell in 1841–42, continued to supply Gould with specimens (including the brilliant finch which Gould named in memory of his wife the Gouldian Painted Finch *Poephila gouldiae*) until his death. He died from spear wounds in 1845; two other collectors were also killed in the field at about this time, one was murdered and the other died in a shooting accident. However, the material they supplied was sufficient to provide a supplement to *Birds of Australia*. The seven volumes of the original work appeared between 1840–48 and contained 600 plates, while the supplement, which was issued some years later, contained a further eighty-one plates.

It was with *Birds of Australia* that Gould refined the classic plate design that is automatically linked with his name. Still using Lear's folio-size format, Gould depicted the male and the female of the species unless they were so similar that he replaced them with frontal and rear views of the birds. The background was simplified to little more than a blue wash suggestive of sky, while the foregrounds could be quite elaborate depending on the type of terrain which was the bird's natural habitat; plants which were important to the bird as food were shown in considerable detail and, if the composition demanded it, the nest, eggs, or chicks might be included. Composition was of vital importance to Gould, who believed that the visual quality of his plates was as essential to their success as the scientific record that was contained within them.

Richter worked closely with Gould on further important volumes: *A Monograph of the Odontophorinae, or Partridges of America* (1844–50), *A Monograph of the Trochilidae, or family of Humming-birds* (1849–60) possibly Gould's most visually pleasing work, and *The Birds of Asia* (1850–83) [see pages 94–99]. However, the latter was unfinished at the time of Gould's death and was completed by his friend Dr Bowdler Sharpe with the help of William Hart. Hart gradually took over more of Gould's lithographic work; he and Richter provided plates for *The Birds of Great Britain* which was issued in twenty-five parts between 1862–73. Wolf contributed a number of water-colours to this work as he also did to *Birds of Asia*; the Gould-Richter partnership tailed off during the 1870s but it had covered thirty of the most productive years of the great naturalist's life.

As ornithologist, publisher, and organizer Gould was without equal; he was described by Josef Wolf as 'a shrewd old fellow, but the most uncouth man I ever knew'. From the mid-1870s he was in failing health, but still managed to oversee the initial work on *The Birds of New Guinea and the Adjacent Papuan Islands*, which he used as a vehicle to place on record all the new species discovered since the publication of *Birds of Australia*. This, like Gould's other unfinished works, was completed by Dr Sharpe. Gould died on 3 February 1881, and much of his life's work passed to the British Museum, including his fantastic collection of humming-birds, although his Australian specimens had already been sold to America.

Satyr Tragopan

Tragopan satyra

A Century of Birds was Gould's first published work, and shows how quickly he responded to the opportunities created by Audubon and Lear during the previous five years. *Illustrations of the family Psittacidae* was still not completed when Gould stepped in and adopted Lear's format of folio-size plates for the presentation of his work; he also followed Lear's example and employed Charles Hullmandel to print the plates. The bird skins which formed the material for this work came from the hills of northern India, although their immediate source was not disclosed nor how they actually came into Gould's possession; what is known is that they came to Gould for stuffing and mounting. Gould immediately realized the value of such a collection and made rough sketches of the birds; these sketches were then worked up by his wife, who also prepared the lithographs.

   With the percipience and flair that was one of his outstanding characteristics, having failed to find a publisher, he decided to publish the material himself. Gould was aware of Lear's struggle to find 175 subscribers for his work on the parrot family, and so he set out to find nearly twice as many; the list is headed by William IV and his Queen, the Duke of Sussex, the Dowager Landgravine of Hesse and Hambourg, and King Leopold I of the Netherlands, and the work is tactfully dedicated 'To their most gracious Majesties William the fourth and Adelaide, King and Queen of the United Kingdoms of Great Britain and Ireland'. The work not only set the pattern for all of Gould's publications, but also for the type of partnership that he was to develop with artists and lithographers – first of all with his wife and then with Richter and Hart.

A Century of Birds hitherto unfigured, from the Himalayan Mountains (1832) plate 62

Citron-throated Toucan

Ramphastos citreolaemus

Unlike the skins of the birds from northern India, which came as a collection and formed the material for *A Century of Birds*, the various species of the Toucan family were sought out by Gould and the drawings assembled for the *Monograph of the Ramphastidae*. Lear had pioneered the idea of devoting an entire work to a single genus; and, obviously, the more spectacular the birds the greater the chance of success with the publication.

The bird depicted in this plate was supplied by fellow ornithologist William Swainson (see pages 52–54) and had never been depicted before; Gould says of it 'For this fine and hitherto uncharacterised species of Toucan, my warmest thanks are due to W. Swainson, Esq. in whose valuable collection it is deposited, and who most liberally placed it at my disposal for the purpose of figuring, and at the same time allowed me to add a specific name of my own authority'. The note continues to the effect that Swainson had purchased it from a Mr Bullock, who reported that the species was native to Peru. Gould named the species the Lemon-rumped Toucan, *Ramphastos citropygus*, but probably due to Victorian prudery the name was later changed and it is now known as the Citron-throated Toucan; certain regions of the body could not be named decently even in relation to the name of a bird! According to the subscript, the plate was drawn from nature, but this probably denotes a stuffed skin rather than a live specimen.

A Monograph of the Ramphastidae or family of Toucans (1833–35) plate 4

GuyanaToucanet

Selenidera culik

The Koulik Aracari, as Gould terms this species, is an inhabitant of 'the rich countries of Cayenne and Guiana' and it is supposed to have derived the name of Koulik from the peculiarity of its cry. The plate shows the male bird in the foreground and the female on the branch above; Gould says 'The male is remarkable for his black breast and the semilunar band between the shoulders, and the female for the chaste colouring of her breast and under parts'. Gould used the *Monograph of the Ramphastidae* to delineate a number of newly found species of Toucan, which obviously aroused the interests of scientists and public alike. The Toucans are strange and ungainly birds, but Gould described the Guyana Toucanet as an 'interesting and elegant species'. The entire work was dedicated to the great Dutch ornithologist, Professor Conrad Temminck of the Leyden Museum, after whom Temminck's Roller (see page 96) was named.

As with *A Century of Birds*, the drawing and lithography was carried out by John and Elizabeth Gould and the printing by Charles Hullmandel. However, in the short time that had elapsed between the publication of the Himalayan birds and commencement of the *Monograph of the Ramphastidae*, a big stride had already been made in presentation. With Lear's book on parrots and Gould's earlier work only the figures of the birds were coloured, but in these plates, with his conception of them as works of art, essential foliage and other integral details were also picked out and unified with the birds, rather than being treated purely as supports.

A Monograph of the Ramphastidae or family of Toucans (1833–35) plate 28

Galapagos Short-eared Owl

Asio flammeus galapogoensis

The second volume of Charles Darwin's *Zoology of the Voyage of H.M.S. Beagle* was devoted to the birds collected on the voyage. Darwin says 'when I presented my collection of birds to the Zoological Society, Mr Gould kindly undertook to furnish me with descriptions of the new species and names for those already known. This he has performed, but owing to the hurry, consequent on his departure for Australia, – an expedition from which the science of Ornithology will derive such great advantages, – he was compelled to leave some part of his manuscript so far incomplete, that without the possibility of personal communication with him, I was left in doubt of some essential points'. This delicately phrased note of thanks points Darwin's problem of dealing with an imperious and busy artist and ornithologist in the days before quick and reliable forms of communication were developed. The Goulds departed for Australia just at the time Darwin's publication was beginning to appear, so the problems of clarification of Gould's manuscript notes must have been considerable, however, GR Gray, of the British Museum stepped in to both elucidate and amplify Gould's notes.

Lear had also worked for Darwin providing illustrations for the *Zoology of of the Voyage of H.M.S. Beagle*, and although the Galapagos Short-eared Owl is similar in treatment to a number of Lear's plates, all the fifty illustrations in this volume are described as 'taken from sketches by Mr Gould himself, and executed on stone by Mrs Gould'.

The Zoology of the Voyage of H.M.S. Beagle under the Command of Captain Fitzroy 1832–36, Charles Darwin (Smith Elder & Co., 1838–41), Volume XI, plate 3

Australian Black-shouldered Kite

Elanus notatus

Abandoning Darwin to sort out his manuscript notes relating to *The Zoology of the Voyage of H.M.S. Beagle*, Gould and his wife left for Australia where Elizabeth's two brothers, Charles and Stephen Coxen, had settled. From the specimens sent home by the Coxens, Gould had already produced *A Synopsis of the Birds of Australia and the Adjacent Islands*, but once in Australia he and his assistant, John Gilbert, carried out a number of exploratory expeditions. The Black-shouldered Kite depicted in this plate was normally regarded as a summer visitor to the southern portions of the Australian continent; however, Gould shot a young bird in New South Wales, which he states had clearly been born and reared in the region where it was killed.

Unlike most species of Falcon, the Black-shouldered Kite is not really a predator; its bill and legs are comparatively feeble, and it lives mainly on insects. Gould gives a vivid account of the species: 'I very often observed it flying above the tops of the highest trees, and where it appeared to be hawking about for insects; it was also sometimes to be seen perched upon the dead and leafless branches of the gums, particularly such as were isolated from other trees of the forest, whence it could survey all around'.

The birds figured in this plate are a male and a female, which are shown life-size in the original lithograph transferred to the stone by Henry Constantine Richter, who took on the lithographic work of *Birds of Australia* after Elizabeth Gould's death in 1841.

Birds of Australia (1840–48) Volume I, plate 23

Budgerigar

Melopsittacus undulatus

Gould's Budgerigars are considerably more lifelike than Lear's (see page 60), but as we know that it was Gould himself who managed to bring the first live specimens to England, when he and Elizabeth returned from Australia in 1840, he must also be the first artist to have drawn one from life rather than from a skin. Nowadays Budgerigars are the most common species of the parrot family to be seen throughout the world, as they have become very popular cage-birds; Gould's brother-in-law, Charles Coxen, managed successfully to rear several birds and it was two of these that reached England.

In his note to this plate Gould realized his advantage and described the bird in glowing terms as being pre-eminent among the numerous members of the parrot family 'for beauty of plumage and elegance of form, which together with its extreme cheerfulness of disposition and sprightliness of manner, render it an especial favourite with all who have an opportunity of seeing it alive'. He noted their habit of breeding in the hollow spouts of eucalyptus trees, and described their migratory habits, which brought large flocks of them to the southern grasslands of Australia in the spring, returning northwards after the breeding season. Their reliance on grass-seed for food is well illustrated in his plate, which figures an old and a young bird natural size.

The preparation of drawings and lithographic plates for *Birds of Australia* was clearly related to the availability of specimens rather than to the plan of the work; this plate, even though it appeared in one of the later volumes, was lithographed by Elizabeth Gould, while the Black-shouldered Kite from Volume I, illustrated on the previous page, was lithographed at a later date by Richter.

Birds of Australia (1840–48) Volume V, plate 44

Cockatiel

Nymphicus hollandicus

Gould called this bird a Cockatoo Parrakeet, *Nymphicus novaeholandicus*; it is an inhabitant of the central parts of Australia, which in the late 1830s was still largely unexplored. For Gould and his associates, it was particularly rewarding terrain since not only was it unknown country, but also, it yielded a fauna peculiarly its own, thus supplying him with a rich harvest of specimens that had not previously been recorded.

Like the Budgerigar in the previous plate, the Cockatiel is a migratory bird; Gould noted that in September the Cockatiels moved towards the Swan River in Western Australia, where they would breed, returning northwards in February and March. Due to its stamina and ability to fly long distances, the bird had occasionally crossed the mountain ranges and been seen near the coast, so it was not totally unknown. Again, it was a numerous species, and he records that it was 'not unusual to see hundreds together on the dead branches of the gum trees in the neighbourhood of water, a plentiful supply of which would appear to be essential to its existence'. Like the Budgerigar it also favoured holes in the gum trees for breeding purposes.

Clearly the notes to this plate were written as a result of first-hand observation, but the drawing was presumably already in existence before the Goulds ever left England for Australia in 1838, since it was executed by Edward Lear from two living specimens in the possession of the Countess of Mountcharles; the birds figured were a male and a female depicted natural size. The lithography was done by Elizabeth Gould, which also indicates that it was one of the earlier plates to be prepared even though it appeared in Volume V.

Birds of Australia (1840–48) Volume V, plate 45

Blue-tailed Bee-eater

Merops philippinus

Birds of Asia was Gould's most protracted publication; he started issuing it in parts in 1850 and it was finally completed in 1883, two years after Gould's death, by his friend Dr Bowdler Sharpe. The complete work, like *Birds of Australia*, runs to seven volumes but contains slightly fewer plates than its Australian counterpart. The earlier parts, including the three plates reproduced here, were lithographed by Richter but William Hart took over midway through publication.

With *Birds of Australia* Gould wrote spirited and well-observed notes, but the text of *Birds of Asia* is more cautious and relied on frequent and extensive notes – always scrupulously acknowledged – from travellers who knew the Indian continent and the many adjacent islands. These informants were often army officers or else government officials. The notes on the Blue-tailed Bee-eater 'one of the most showy and attractive birds of its native forests' were written by a Mr Jerdon. The species was listed as being generally dispersed over the Indian subcontinent, Ceylon, Malaya, Singapore, Java, Sumatra, and the Philippines, from where it takes its name. 'It is almost always found in small parties seated on the tops of high trees, frequently among wet paddy-fields' reported Jerdon 'I once saw an immense flock of them at Caroor . . . in the beginning of March, there were many thousands of them perched on the lofty trees lining the road there, which sallied forth for half an hour or so, making a great circuit before returning'. The object of this circuit was to collect insects after the manner of swallows; with the approach of the hot season the Bee-eaters migrate northwards to more wooded regions. The call of the species was described as a loud and pleasing sort of whistle 'but more full and mellow'.

Birds of Asia (1850–83) Volume I, plate 36

Temminck's Roller

Coracias temminckii

Temminck's Roller is a native of the Celebes, Moluccas, and Macassar; it is an exotic bird of brightly coloured plumage of which Gould says 'It rarely happens that one of the finest species of a *genus* is selected to bear the name of a scientific man as its specific designation; but such is the case in the present instance; for it may be truly said that not a finer species of *coracias* has yet been discovered'. The scientist after whom this species was named was Professor Conrad Joseph Temminck, one of the most distinguished men in the whole field of natural history and director of the museum at Leyden; Gould had met Temminck in the 1830s but, curiously, no hint of personal friendship comes through his otherwise glowing tribute which accompanies this plate. Gould describes Temminck as 'a Dutch gentleman who lived in the latter part of the eighteenth and the early part of the nineteenth centuries, who devoted his whole life and much of his private fortune to the advancement of science and ornithology, and under whose direction and fostering care the fine Museum at Leyden was rendered so rich in zoological stores as scarcely to be surpassed, if equalled, by any other in existence'.

It was probably as an additional tribute to the Dutch ornithologist that Gould lavished such attention on this plate; the two birds, figured life-size, are depicted perched on the branch of a Hoya, *Hoya fraterna*, sharing a tasty meal, which is identified as *Hyla reinwardtii*.

The lithographer is named in the subscript as Walton, who had joined Hullmandel as an assistant.

Birds of Asia (1850–83) Volume I, plate 56

Black and Red Broadbill

Cymbirhynchus macrorhynchus

This species, which Gould termed the Great-billed Eurylaime, is a native of Sumatra, the Malayan peninsula, and Malacca. 'From its singular structure and rich colouring few of the birds of Tropical India are more conspicuous and interesting.' Some of the notes for this plate were supplied by Sir Stamford Raffles, who told Gould that the species was found in the interior of Sumatra, where it frequented the banks of rivers and lakes which provided its main diet of insects and worms.

The two specimens depicted were believed by Gould to be male and female; in this instance, in addition to the skins, he was also working from a drawing in the possession of the London office of the East India Company. Gould states the belief that the beautiful hues of the bill and legs of this species fade almost immediately after death, and quotes as evidence of this the difference between the drawing belonging to the East India Company, which was made from life, and the preserved specimens that had reached England. The drawing which he consulted he said was 'well executed' and showed the soft parts of the species; he goes on to say that 'having been made in India, [it] may, I presume be depended upon'. Presumably no nest had accompanied the specimens which appear in the plate, because, from Raffles's account, it sounds interesting and picturesque and would almost certainly have tempted Gould to draw it if it had been available; the species 'builds its nest pendent from the branch of a tree or bush which overhangs the water'.

Like the two previous illustrations this plate was lithographed by Richter, but in this case the credit for printing is given jointly to Hullmandel and Walton.

Birds of Asia (1850–83) Volume I, plate 59

New Guinea Harpy Eagle

Harpyopsis novaeguineae

This five-volume work, which bears the cumbersome title of *The Birds of New Guinea and the adjacent Papuan Islands including many new species recently discovered in Australia*, was only half finished at the time of Gould's death and was completed by his old friend, Richard Bowdler Sharpe, who wrote the note to the plate of the New Guinea Harpy Eagle.

Gould had always used colaborators and William Hart, who had been his principal artist for some years, was involved from the beginning with *The Birds of New Guinea*; the plate of the Harpy Eagle is described as having been both drawn and lithographed by Hart, but, presumably, the initial sketches were by Gould himself. In a long note to the plate Sharpe says 'This magnificent bird of prey is one of the most important and at the same time one of the most interesting of all the discoveries made by Signor D'Albertis during his travels in New Guinea. It is a veritable Harpy, like the Harpy Eagle of South America (*Thrasaetus harpyia*), which it so closely resembles in outward form that we had great difficulty in finding characters for its generic separation from the South-American bird. It has the crest differently formed to that of the true Harpy, and the wing is shorter in proportion to the length of the tail; but there can be no doubt that the two forms are intimately allied. How such a close similarity has been obtained between two Eagles inhabiting such widely different localities as South America and New Guinea, the avifaunae of which have, generally speaking, very little in common, is a problem of geographical distribution which our present knowledge has no means of explaining'.

The Birds of New Guinea (Henry Sotheran & Co., 1875–88) Volume I, plate 3

Arfak Astrapia

Astrapia nigra

With his possessive interest in Australian birdlife, which he was largely responsible for introducing to European audiences, Gould did not wish to relinquish his hold on that continent, and *The Birds of New Guinea* provided him with a convenient work to which he could add such new species as had been discovered since 1848, when the last part of *The Birds of Australia* was published.

Gould termed the birds in this plate Gorget Paradise-birds, and described at length the problems ornithologists had to contend with in defining the limits of the family *paradiseidae*; in his experience only two other groups presented the same obstacles to classification, namely Hornbills and Malkoha Cuckoos. All five species of *Astrapia* are restricted to the Arfak Mountains of New Guinea, where they live at altitudes between 5000–7000 feet; Gould records that one of his informants, Dr Beccari, had shot several of these birds which 'are only found on the highest and most difficult peaks of Mount Arfak, nearly always above 6000 feet elevation'. 'The figures are drawn from specimens in my own collection, and represent a male about the size of life, with reduced figures of a male and female in the distance.' The elaboration and sophistication of this plate is far removed from the stilted simplicity of Havell's *Birds of Paradise* (see page 50) of less than half a century earlier.

The lithography for *The Birds of New Guinea* was carried out by William Hart, and, as with Gould's other uncompleted works, the later parts were edited by his friend Dr Richard Bowdler Sharpe.

The Birds of New Guinea (Henry Sotheran & Co., 1875–88) Volume I, plate 17

Josef Wolf

1820–1899

Josef Wolf, 'The Bird Man' from Möerz in Prussia, was the first of a select band of continental European bird and animal artists to be attracted to England during the middle and latter half of the nineteenth century – Smit, Keulemans, and Grönvold were to follow suit. Born on 21 January 1820, in the village of Möerz near Coblenz, the son of a farmer and local headman, young Josef was regarded as something of an oddity by his family and friends as he slipped away to watch and trap birds, try his hand at drawing, or walk the twenty miles to Neuwied to observe the rare South American birds collected by Prince Maximillian. He was also regarded as an idler for, like other boys of his age, he was expected to work hard on his father's farm. At the age of sixteen he left home and apprenticed himself for three years to the lithographic firm of Gebruder Becker in Coblenz; this training as a lithographer was not only to gain him the grudging respect of his family and to stand him in good stead throughout his life, but also to assist, at least in part, in getting him his first important commission from Hermann Schlegel, a fellow countryman who was at that time assistant keeper at the museum in Leyden. Schlegel, no mean artist himself, was a prolific author and advocate of lithography as the best and most direct process for the illustration of ornithological works.

After brief spells in Frankfurt and Darmstadt, Wolf went to Holland and settled in Leyden in 1840; he was soon at work on the illustrations for *Traité de Fauconnerie* (see page 106) by Schlegel and Wulverhorst. The collaboration with Schlegel was to continue over several years as the *Traité de Fauconnerie* was followed by *Birds of Japan* (see pages 108 and 110) which formed part of von Siebold's *Fauna Japonica*. The success of these plates did not satisfy Wolf, who still felt he had much to learn, so in 1847 he enrolled as a student of painting at the Antwerp Academy. Wolf's big break came when Dr Kaup visited England bringing some of the artist's studies with him, which resulted in John Gould commissioning directly a watercolour of partridges; realizing the importance of this commission and also the potential market for his work in England, Wolf moved to London in 1848.

He quickly established himself in London, exhibited at the Royal Academy – his first exhibit there in 1849, *Woodcocks seeking Shelter*, had been commissioned by Gould – made contacts with Edwin Landseer and other animal artists, and also with influential patrons like the Duke of Argyll and Lord Derby. The rapidity of the growth of his reputation was due, according to his biographer AH Palmer, to his power 'of revivifying a dried skin and not merely revivifying, but showing the most characteristic and beautiful attitude and

expression of the living bird or animal'. This in turn was due to the fact that as a boy he had spent a lot of time studying the attitudes of birds, both at rest and in flight, in the woodlands and heathlands near his father's farm, and had realized at an early age that the stance and flight of a bird were as distinctive as its markings.

Wolf had an amused respect for Gould and contributed plates to both *The Birds of Asia* and *The Birds of Great Britain*, and Gould became a frequent although not always welcome visitor to Wolf's studio; in 1856 the two artists travelled together through Norway. By the early 1850s Wolf was already held in such repute that PL Sclater, writing the preface to *Zoological Sketches* (First Series), was able to say 'In the year 1852 the Council of the Zoological Society, impressed with the sense of the great value of an artistic record of the living form and expression of the many rare species of animals which exist from time to time in the menagerie, resolved to commence the formation of a series of original water-colour drawings to illustrate the most interesting of these subjects. For this purpose the Council was fortunate enough to secure the services of Mr Joseph Wolf, who may be fairly said to stand alone in intimate knowledge of the habits and forms of Mammals and Birds'. A selection of the original watercolours was reproduced in the two series of *Zoological Sketches* (see page 112) published in parts between 1856–67.

By this stage in his career, Wolf's watercolours were in considerable demand both in their own right and as illustrations to books and journals; from 1859–69 he was the regular artist for *Ibis* the journal of the Zoological Society, and his work was also reproduced in the *Illustrated London News*, *Once a Week*, *The Leisure Hour*, *The Sunday at Home*, and *The Graphic*, so it is not surprising that the job of transferring his watercolour drawings onto the lithographic stone gradually passed to other artists. Wolf was not always happy with the results that these lithographers produced and on one occasion, while looking at a very curious sky that had found its way into one of these lithographs, he remarked 'And then they did the clouds you see; one – two – three – four! They weren't even asked for that'. However, in some cases he was luckier; JG Keulemans was employed to transfer the watercolours for Elliot's *A Monograph of the Phasianeidae* (see pages 118–123), a combination that was particularly successful since Keulemans had a penchant for bright colours, while Wolf, one of the greatest bird artists of the nineteenth century, was most completely at home with the more muted colouring of the birds of prey. Unfortunately, during the 1870s, Wolf was increasingly hindered by the onset of chronic rheumatism, which gradually curtailed his work, but he lived on into his eightieth year and died in London surrounded by his pet birds and held in high popular esteem. More than three-quarters of a century later his plates are regarded as among the finest productions of the great period of the illustrated book, while his watercolours and drawings are prized by museums and collectors alike.

Gyrfalcon

Falco rusticolus

This plate is one of a dozen hand-coloured lithographs contributed by Wolf to Schlegel's great treatise on falconry. The book, dedicated to King William III of Holland, has a French language text despite being published in Leyden. Dr Hermann Schlegel (1804–84) who was to become director of the Musée d'Histoire Naturelle des Pays-Bas at Leyden was, like Wolf, a German. The book was inspired by the formation of a falconry club at the royal castle of Loo, which once again raised falconry to the position of a sport of kings and princes, a status it had not enjoyed since the Middle Ages. In addition to Wolf's plates, the book contains two plates by MJB Sonderland depicting a falconry party on heathland near Loo in which the Dutch King, Prince Alexander and the Duke of Leeds are active participants; these two plates are entitled 'The Flight of the Heron', and it is against herons that the falcons are matched in skill and speed – the bag of dead herons testifies to the quality of the sport. There are two further plates by Portman and van Wouw, which show in detail the trappings of the falcon and the instruments required by the falconer.

This plate showing the gyrfalcon with its beautiful feathered hood like some large and exotic fishing fly, bells and fetters, represents the traditional romantic image of the manly sport of falconry; the powerful gloved hand controlling the fierce bird of prey. The other plates contributed by Wolf show the birds in their wild state and natural habitats; although equally fine as far as draughts-manship and execution are concerned they do not have the power to thrill in the way that the hooded falcon does.

Wolf's interest in birds of prey started in boyhood with the observations he made in the countryside around Möerz, and throughout his life his depictions of predators were full of sympathy and understanding. It was probably the illustrations to *Traité de Fauconnerie* which recommended him to Johann Susemihl, who almost immediately commissioned Wolf to draw the owls and falcons for his book on European birds – *Abbildungen der Vogel Europas* (1846–52).

Traité de Fauconnerie by Hermann Schlegel and AH Verster de Wulverhorst (Arnz et Comp., Leyden, 1844–1853)

Dessiné par M. WOLF.

LE GROENLANDAIS, FAUCON BLANC MUÉ.

Ural Owl

Strix uralensis

Siebold had compiled both the *Flora Japonica* and *Fauna Japonica*, the latter during the 1820s, but it was not edited and published until the 1840s. The editing was done by Wolf's friend Hermann Schlegel and his ageing colleague from Leyden, the grand old man of Dutch ornithology, Professor Conrad Temminck. Wolf's work had originally been shown to Schlegel by Dr Kaup, director of the museum at Darmstadt, during an ornithological conference in Leyden. Wolf subsequently went to Leyden and met Schlegel for whom he made plates to illustrate the *Traité de Fauconnerie* (see page 106); no doubt at the same period he also made the acquaintance of Professor Temminck. However, it was after he had returned to Darmstadt that he was commissioned to draw a score of plates for Siebold's *Fauna Japonica*. As with the treatise on falconry, the text for this work is in French; the descriptions of the birds are straight-forward and are stated to be from observations made by 'les voyageurs Hollandais' in Japan. The Dutch had been able to establish a trading base in Japan several centuries before Commander Perry enabled that country to be generally accessible to westerners, hence the emphasis on the fact that the notes were compiled by Dutch travellers, and therefore first-hand.

Wolf had already shown himself to be a masterly draughtsman of the larger predators, and although he was presumably working from skins with the Ural Owl, he had observed in detail sufficient members of the owl family to imbue the bird with life. The impression of vitality both in drawing and in the presentation of specimens was a continuing preoccupation of Wolf's, and Palmer records that he was very scathing of the professional naturalists; 'Those fellows know very little. To put a bird right, they smooth it down with their hands, and tie paper round it very tightly, but this gives a totally false impression. The feathers are naturally full of spring, and lie lightly'.

Fauna Japonica, PF Von Siebold (Apud Arnz & Socios, 1844–50) plate 10

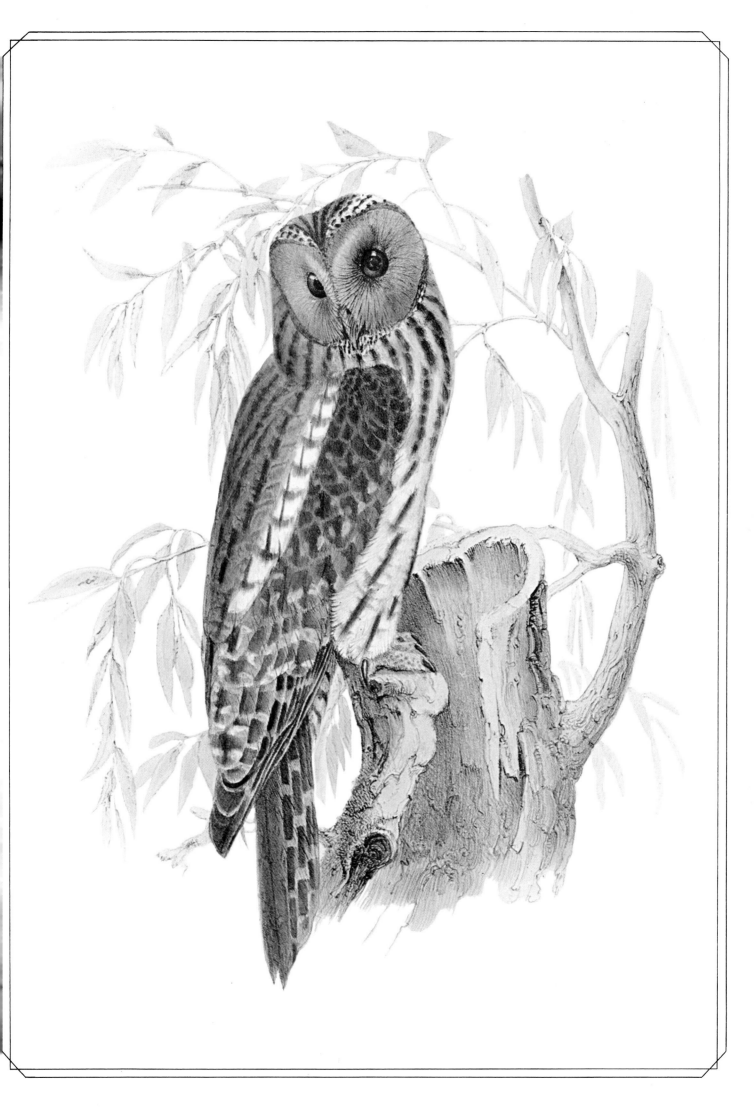

Jungle Nightjar

Caprimulgus indicus

The Jungle Nightjar is widely distributed throughout eastern Asia and India, while the genus *Caprimulgus* is spread throughout most of the world. The Jungle Nightjar differs from its European cousins, most notably in its markings, especially with regard to the number of its tail-feathers which carry the distinctive white discs; the American Chuck-will's-widow figured by Audubon (see page 46) is also of the same family.

HE Dresser, the author of *A History of the Birds of Europe* (see page 114), to whom Schlegel gave one of Wolf's drawings for *Fauna Japonica*, relates an anecdote concerning the first time Schlegel took Wolf to see some birds; the birds were waders and marsh-birds and 'on arriving among them, he (Schlegel) asked Wolf where his note book and pencil were, but the answer was that he did not require them. After spending some time watching the birds, they returned to Leyden, and Schlegel asked Wolf to supper, for which purpose they adjourned to a restaurant; and, after supper Wolf asked for paper and pencil, and made some excellent sketches of birds he had that day seen for the first time'. This story, which is relayed by Wolf's biographer, not only tells something about the basis of the collaboration between Schlegel and Wolf, but also indicates the powers of observation and memory that the artist had cultivated. It was his capacity for near total recall which enabled him to draw away from the subject, and thus capture attitudes and movement that were characteristic of the birds and animals he was figuring.

By the time the final parts of *Fauna Japonica* were issued, Wolf had left the continent for London; although only thirty years old he had already established a considerable reputation, not only in his native country, but also in Holland and England, which, for ornithologists, were the two leading countries of Europe.

Fauna Japonica, PF Von Siebold (Apud Arnz & Socios, 1844–50) plate 12

African Wood Ibis

Ibis ibis

Zoological Sketches was issued in two series, the first in 1856 and the second twelve years later; the second series includes this plate of the African Wood Ibis, which is followed by a plate of the Indian Wood Ibis. At the time of publication the wood ibis family was still an exotic and little known genus, although the ordinary ibis was well known. Philip Lutley Sclater, the secretary of the Zoological Society, who wrote the notes for *Zoological Sketches* – or to give it its full title *Zoological Sketches by Joseph Wolf made for the Zoological Society of London from animals in their Vivarium in the Regent's Park* – says 'The small group of wading birds to which Linnaeus gave the name of *Tantalus* is closely allied to the Storks, although most writers on Natural History have hitherto associated them with the Ibises. But while many species of the latter group are very commonly met with in the Zoological Gardens of Europe, the Wood Ibises (as the *Tantali* are usually called) are birds of greater rarity, and are seldom seen in our Aviaries. In the Summer of 1865, however, the Zoological Society were fortunate enough to possess living pairs of two species of this scarce form, which from their quaint outlines and beautiful plumage, attracted much attention. Mr Wolf has illustrated the various attitudes they assume in this and the next succeeding plate'. The next plate is, of course, of the second species referred to, namely the Indian Wood Ibis. These plates are far more complex and pictorial than anything attempted by Gould; Wolf's intention, as Sclater says, was not only to depict the bird factually, but also to illustrate the various attitudes characteristic to the species.

 Zoological Sketches is not restricted to birds; each series contains fifty plates by Wolf, and those in the second series illustrate a wide variety of animals including a lemur, the Norwegian Lynx, various species of deer, and several different brightly coloured hornbills.

Zoological Sketches (Henry Graves & Co., 1867) plate 46

Great Grey Owl

Strix nebulosa

As with so many other species, the name of this owl has been changed during the century which has elapsed since Henry Dresser published *The Birds of Europe*; to him and to Wolf it was the Lapp Owl, *Syrnium lapponicum*. Its old name immediately pinpoints the geographical region from which the bird came. According to Dresser it was one of the rarest owls inhabiting the Palaearctic region; its breeding ground was confined to the wooded regions along the Swedish and Finnish borders, and its natural habitat was the upper portion of the forest belt. It rarely straggled down even into what he termed the northern portions of Europe. There is no indication of whether Dresser had ever actually seen the bird in its natural habitat, but we know from the note that the adult bird depicted in this plate was in his own collection, while the young one was supplied by Dr Finsch.

With Wolf's exceptional talent for depicting owls, it is surprising that the other owl plates in *The Birds of Europe* are all autolithographs by Keulemans, including two beautiful plates of the Snowy Owl. Wolf was no longer working as a lithographer by this time, and his watercolour was transferred to the stone by Gould's old collaborator, William Hart.

The Birds of Europe, HE Dresser (1871–81), Volume V, plate 309

Siberian Spruce Grouse

Dendrophagus falcipennis

Daniel Giraud Elliot, the American ornithologist, published a number of monographs devoted to different families of birds, and after detailing the grouse turned to the pheasants (see pages 118–123); his choice was influenced at least in part by the pleasures of sport and delights of the table, as is indicated in his introduction to the present volume. 'Although not so brilliant or attractive in their plumage as the Pheasants, yet, in consequence of the delicacy of their flesh, the Grouse are valuable birds, and in the bleak regions of the frozen north, the Ptarmigan are one of the chief means of subsistence for the inhabitants, who kill thousands of them annually, and salt their flesh for the winter's consumption. Perhaps no family of birds, excepting the Phasianidae, contains species of so much importance to man, as those comprising this monograph, whether considered as affording him food, or as objects of sport in the field.' Elliot, however, was first and foremost an ornithologist and it fell to him during the 1860s to give this species its specific name. He did not classify it with the *Dendrophagus*, but put it in a separate category *Falcipennis* giving it the specific name of *hartlaubii*, in honour of Dr Hartlaub whom he says was the first person to note the differences between this bird and the Spruce Grouse. History seems to have largely reversed this judgement and deprived the doctor of his prize.

Although the plate is not one of Wolf's most sympathetic renderings, he does manage to convey something of the stolid quality, which enables the species to survive in the bitter regions of Siberia, its natural habitat.

A Monograph of the Tetraoninae or family of the Grouse, DG Elliot (New York, 1865), plate 11

Blyth's Tragopan

Tragopan blythii

The two volumes of *A Monograph of the Phasianeidae* by the American naturalist Daniel Giraud Elliot (1835–1915) are among the most oppulent bird books produced. AH Palmer, in his biography of Wolf, calculates that the illustrations to the *Phasianeidae* run to 246 square feet, and says the volumes form 'an *edition de luxe*; that is to say they in every way promote the discomfort of the would-be reader; who, in heaving them up upon the table, involuntarily wishes that the author's expenses had not been quite so liberally allowed'. Palmer's attitude is unnecessarily puritanical.

The Blyth's Tragopan illustrated in this plate was described as having been so recently discovered 'that nothing is yet known regarding its habits'. The species had just been described by Dr Sclater of the Zoological Society in the Society's *Proceedings*, and Elliot felt he could do no better than to quote Sclater, who reported that 'In October last Dr TC Jerdon, the well-known Indian naturalist, addressed to me a letter from Shillong, a new sanitarium on the Khasya Hills in Upper Assam, stating that he had obtained from the hill-ranges in the neighbourhood of Suddya a skin of a Tragopan (ceriornis), distinct from either of the well-known Indian species'. The birds depicted by Wolf and which had reached Regent's Park safely, were supplied by a Major Montagu of the Bengal Staff Corps. Sclater was particularly interested in the manner in which the male paid his addresses to the female of the species; 'when approaching her, he lowers all the feathers which are on the side nearest to her, almost hiding his legs, showing to the greatest advantage all the beautiful markings of his plumage, and the admirable manner in which the colours blend into one another'.

A Monograph of the Phasianeidae, or family of the Pheasants, DG Elliot (New York, 1872) Volume 1, plate 26

Himalayan Monal

Lephophorus impejanus

Elliot acted as his own publisher for the *Phasianeidae*, which he issued from his address at 27 West Thirty Third Street, New York. The whole work glows with the rich colouring of the plumage of the many bright and exotic species of pheasant; however, Elliot says that of the three known species of the genus *Lephophorus* the Himalayan Monal, reproduced here, is entitled to carry the palm for beauty. The species had been known in Europe for some years, and Lord Derby had had a pair of them in his aviary at Knowsley as early as 1846; by the time *A Monograph of the Phasianeidae* was being compiled, Elliot states that they were a familiar sight in nearly every zoological garden in Europe. He says 'At the period I write, May 1870, there is a male in the gardens of the Society in Regent's Park in the finest plumage I have ever witnessed; and it is quite impossible by any plate to do full justice to the magnificent appearance of the species'. As its name implies, the species is found in the Himalayas, throughout the entire range; although the author was familiar with various zoo specimens, he relied on a report extracted from the *Bengal Sporting Review* for details of its behaviour when in its natural habitat. The anonymous writer records that 'from April to the commencement of the cold season, the Monal is rather wild and shy; but this soon gives way to the all-taming influence of winter's frosts and snows'.

From the time he came to England, Wolf concentrated almost entirely on his watercolours and drawings and delegated the lithography to others; for *A Monograph of the Phasianeidae* much of the lithography, including this plate, was carried out by John Gerrard Keulemans, another protégé of Schlegel's who had recently come to England.

A Monograph of the Phasianeidae, or family of the Pheasants, DG Elliot (New York, 1872), Volume I, plate 18

Common Pheasant

Phasianus colchicus

Elliot called this bird the Ringless Chinese Pheasant, *Phasianus deccolatus*, in contrast to the one depicted by Wolf as plate 6 of the monograph, which was the Formosan Pheasant with its distinctive white collar. The Ringless species had only been discovered three years before this publication, and Elliot quotes Mr Swinhoe's account of his voyage up the Yangtze river in which he says 'on the 13th of May, 1869, the day after our arrival at Chungkingfoo in Szechuan, the servant returned from the market with this Pheasant. He fortunately showed it to me before he handed it to the cook. I was at once struck by the absence of the collar, and tried to get more specimens, but without success. The natives declared that they had never seen the Pheasant with the white collar'. Despite the lapse of only three years, other specimens had been sent to the Jardin des Plantes by a French missionary, Père David, who had found them at Moupin near the Tibetan border. Of these Elliot reported 'the examples procured by Père David differ slightly from Mr Swinhoe's type; and I have therefor represented the Moupin style of this Pheasant by the sitting figure in this plate. They are undoubtedly of the same race'.

The species which Elliot called the Common Pheasant was figured as plate 2 in this volume, and with his interest in the table it is quite characteristic that he should have noted the fact that the Pheasant had been known in England at least since the eleventh century, since it featured on a bill of fare for the Canon's household at Waltham in 1059.

A Monograph of the Phasianeidae or family of the Pheasants, DG Elliot (New York, 1872) Volume II, plate 7

Joseph Smit

1836–1929

Smit was a Dutchman, born at Lisse in Holland on 18 July 1836; little is known about the circumstances of his childhood and early life, but clearly it involved a study of birds and animals in the countryside around Lisse, and presumably some formal artistic training. Like Wolf before him, Smit was attracted to Leyden where he met Professor Hermann Schlegel, whose patronage was so important to a number of natural history draughtsmen; at no time was this more important than at the beginning of their careers. He gave Smit his first commission, which was to transfer his own drawings to the stone to illustrate *De Vogels van Nederlandsch Indie*, which was published between 1863–66. It is interesting to note that while Schlegel immediately entrusted Wolf with both illustration and lithography, in the case of Smit it was lithography only. From Leyden, Smit moved to London at the suggestion of Philip Lutley Sclater of the Zoological Society, with whom he was already in touch; he illustrated Sclater's *Exotic Ornithology containing figures and descriptions of new and rare species of American birds* (1866–69), and it is likely that he was already drawing specimens to illustrate this work even before he left Holland.

He moved with his wife and family to London in 1866 when he finished work on Schlegel's lithographic illustrations; production of *Exotic Ornithology*, which was illustrated by 100 hand-coloured lithographs, must have been greatly facilitated by having the artist working in closer proximity to the author. Shortly after making the move to London, Smit met Josef Wolf with whom he found himself in complete sympathy, and the two men struck up a friendship which was to last until Wolf's death at the end of the century. The first fruits of this friendship were the excellent lithographs Smit carried out from Wolf's watercolours for the second series of *Zoological Sketches* (see page 112). Although autolithography had helped Wolf in his early days, as his reputation grew he quickly abandoned the practice of transferring his own work onto the stone, preferring to be free to pursue his career as draughtsman and watercolourist.

The two men worked together again on DG Elliott's *A Monograph of the Phasianeidae* and *A Monograph of the Paradiseidae*, although JG Keulemans was also actively engaged as a lithographer on the first of these two works.

Keulemans, like Smit, was a Dutchman, who had worked for Schlegel before coming to London. During the second half of the nineteenth century there were a number of wealthy naturalists who not only employed collectors in various parts of the world to supply them with specimens, but also financed voyages of exploration, the results of which they then published in well-illustrated volumes. The first such patron for whom Smit worked was the distinguished traveller Julius Lucius Brenchley (1816–73), who had been cruising on HMS Curaçao among the South Sea Islands; he subsequently published his *Jottings*, for which GR Gray described the birds from the specimens he brought back, while Smit provided the illustrations. He also provided illustrations for Arthur Hay (the ninth Marquis of Tweeddale), the president of the Zoological Society, who reprinted from the Society's *Transactions* 'A list of Birds known to inhabit the Philippine Archipeligo'.

Smit's illustrations appeared regularly in both the *Transactions* and *Proceedings of the Zoological Society* as well as in *Ibis*; later, he also adapted to changing demands as well as to new printing technology and contributed to both *The Field* and *Nature*. Another voyage, the report of which Smit illustrated, was that of HMS Challenger, which went round the world engaged on oceanic exploration during 1875–76; it carried a team of scientists under the leadership of the zoologist (Sir) John Murray. The report was edited by various naturalists, with the section on birds being entrusted to Smit's old patron PL Sclater. The biggest work which occupied most of the bird artists in England during the 1870s to the 1890s was the *Catalogue of Birds in the Collection of the British Museum*, which ran to twenty-seven volumes; Smit contributed extensively to this work, being helped at times by his son, Pierre, who also contributed illustrations in his own right. Although Smit was best known in museum circles and never achieved the popular acclaim of his younger contemporaries such as Keulemans and Thorburn, he worked on many publications; during the years he was extensively occupied with the British Museum *Catalogue*, he still managed to find time to contribute to Lord Lilford's *Coloured Figures of the Birds of the British Islands* and to supply the illustrations to Canon Tristram's *The Survey of Western Palestine*.

Smit did not confine his interests to birds alone, but ranged over the whole animal kingdom; during his later years he showed a marked preference for mammals, and after Wolf's death in 1899 he was regarded by many as the best animal artist in Britain. As he lived to extreme old age his output of both watercolours and publications dwindled. He died at the age of ninety-three at Radlett in Hertfordshire in 1929, while his son, Pierre, who had followed in his footsteps, emigrated to South Africa.

Snake Bird

Anhinga rufa

The author of *The Survey of Western Palestine*, Henry Baker Tristram
(1822–1906), was an anglican clergyman; he suffered from incipient lung
trouble, which forced him to leave his living in County Durham for long
spells and visit hot dry countries; during these enforced trips he indulged his
passion for natural history. His first book was entitled *The Great Sahara* (1860);
he subsequently published *The Natural History of the Bible*, which described
every animal and plant mentioned in Holy Scripture, and *The Survey of
Western Palestine*. The latter book was financed and published by the Palestine
Exploration Fund, and an editorial note says that the Committee of the Fund
'which has already contributed so much to the general stock of information as
to the geography, topography, history and archaeology of that country felt
that their work would be incomplete until supplemented by an account of its
natural productions'.

Tristram, who had declined Disraeli's offer of the anglican bishopric in
Jerusalem in 1879, was the ideal person to carry out the survey of the 'natural
productions'. In his note accompanying the plate of the Snake Bird, which he
identified as an African Darter (*Plotus levaillantii*), he said 'though I have not
actually obtained this bird within the confines of Palestine proper, yet, as I
have discovered a great breeding colony on the Lake of Antioch, which the
bird could not possibly have reached without passing through Palestine, I
think it fairly deserves a place here'. Another of the birds depicted by Smit –
Tristram's Grackle – was named after the author; to many of his friends the
author himself bore the name of a bird, being known affectionately as the
'Sacred Ibis'.

The Survey of Western Palestine, HB Tristram (The Committee of the Palestine
Exploration Fund, 1888) plate 13

Syrian Serin and Dead Sea Sparrow

Serinus syriacus (1, female; 2, male), *Passer moabiticus* (3, male; 4, female)

The Syrian Serin used to be known as *Serinus canonicus*, a name given to it in honour of Canon Tristram – the 'Great Gun of Durham' as he was also known – and his work on the natural history of the Bible lands; Henry Dresser refers to the species as Tristram's Serin. Of the bird itself, Tristram says 'this is one of the few interesting peculiar forms of Palestine, though belonging not to the Dead Sea valley, but to the Lebanon and anti-Lebanon exclusively. It is a true Siskin in its habits, note, and nidification. It never migrates, but descends to the villages on the edge of the snow-line in winter, re-ascending as high as there are bushes in spring'. This is typical of Tristram's style, and the use of such words as 'nidification' is entirely characteristic; with regard to the nest he says that it is like that of the Goldfinch, being placed conspicuously in the forked branch of a tall shrub.

The Dead Sea Sparrow was to Tristram an exceedingly rare species; he claimed to have searched for it on three successive expeditions and only been successful on that of 1864. It is the most diminutive member of the sparrow family; a shy wary and restless little bird, of which Tristram says 'so far as our present knowledge extends, this bird is the most limited in the world in its range, and the scarcest in number of individuals. And yet it is marked off from its allies more distinctly than any other member of the genus *Passer*'. The two places that Tristram recorded finding specimens were on the western side of the Dead Sea and again at Ghor es Safieh at the south-eastern end; in both cases he located it among reeds.

The Survey of Western Palestine, HB Tristram (The Committee of the Palestine Exploration Fund, 1888) plate 9

John Gerrard Keulemans

1842–1912

Keulemans was a Dutchman, born in Rotterdam on 8 June 1842; his early professional career followed much the same pattern as Wolf's; he worked for several years at the Leyden Museum, where, like the older artist, he was patronized and encouraged by Professor Hermann Schlegel, who also helped him in the mastery of lithography. Schlegel gave Keulemans his first serious commission, which was to provide illustrations for *Notes from the Leyden Museum*. However, Keulemans wished to travel, and in 1862 he left Leyden and went on a collecting expedition to Africa, visiting the Cape Verde Islands and Principe at the same time; if circumstances had turned out differently he might have, at this stage, abandoned Europe and professional ornithology, but illness was to intervene. While in West Africa he bought a coffee plantation with the intention of settling there, but he contracted a serious bout of fever which forced him to sell the plantation and return to Europe, where once more he found himself working for the Leyden Museum.

Like other protégés of Professor Schlegel he was soon lured away by the outstanding opportunities offered by London, which, with its important Zoological Society had established itself as the centre for ornithological publications. Gould had provided the first commissions for Wolf, which attracted him to London, and it was Gould's friend Richard Bowdler Sharpe who was responsible for luring Keulemans to England in 1869. Sharpe, although only in his early twenties, was already librarian at the Zoological Society and had started work on his *Monograph of the Alcedinidae or family of Kingfishers*; Keulemans had supplied illustrations to the earliest parts before actually moving to London, and it was this work which convinced him to make the change. Almost immediately on arrival in London he was to lithograph a number of Wolf's plates for Elliot's *A Monograph of the Phasianeidae*; he was to work for a number of ornithologists, but his collaboration with Bowdler Sharpe was particularly close and they worked together through three decades. Mrs CE Jackson in her excellent book *Bird Illustrators: some Artists in early Lithography* states 'Any author of a bird-book between 1870 and 1900 requiring an illustrator almost automatically thought first of Keulemans'.

Keulemans was a prodigious and reliable worker. In 1869, while still

working on Sharpe's *Monograph of the Alcedinidae*, he took over from Wolf as the regular illustrator of *Ibis* and his drawings appeared in that publication for the rest of his life; his style and format barely changed during the whole of that period, but he maintained the high standards, which had first attracted the attention of Dr Bowdler Sharpe. Gould, having emulated Lear's folio-size plates, set the pattern which Keulemans followed of representing both sexes of the species on one plate, unless the size of the specimen made this impracticable. He depicted the birds at rest with foliage, fruit, and so on, representative of their typical feeding pattern and habitat; the inclusion or otherwise of nests, eggs, or young was most frequently dictated by aesthetic rather than scientific considerations. Like Gould he worked mostly from skins and Gould actually supplied Sharpe with many of the specimens for his book on the kingfishers.

The area in which he departed from Gouldian precept was in his abilities as a lithographer, which not only enabled him to transfer many of his own drawings to the stone, but also made him a valued collaborator for many other artists, most especially for Josef Wolf. Keulemans executed and lithographed more than 100 plates for the British Museum *Catalogue of Birds* which shows his extraordinary diversity and ability to depict birds of widely different species from parrots to birds of prey. In addition to the kingfishers, he either illustrated or lithographed monographs devoted to barbets, cranes, bee-eaters, rollers, hornbills, petrels, jacamars, puff-birds, sun-birds, and thrushes. His illustrations of birds for works related to geographic regions is equally diverse covering Great Britain, Europe, Abyssinia, Australia, New Zealand, India, South Africa, and Central America. Two works are particularly deserving of attention; these are Sir Walter Buller's *A History of the Birds of New Zealand* (1873) and the earlier volumes of Lord Lilford's *Coloured Figures of the Birds of the British Islands* executed before illness overtook him, and he was replaced by Archibald Thorburn who completed this mammoth task. *Birds of New Zealand* is possibly Keulemans' most beautiful work, although it only contains thirty-six plates by him, of which, in the first edition, thirty-five were hand-coloured by Bowdler Sharpe's three daughters. A number of Keulemans' original watercolours for this work are in the Zoological Museum at Tring, now a part of the British Museum (Natural History). Tring was originally Lord Rothschild's private zoological museum, where he assembled specimens supplied by his collectors in Polynesia and the Malay Archipelago; the reports of these finds appeared in the journal *Novitates Zoologicae* and were illustrated by Keulemans, who also supplied many of the plates for Lord Rothschild's *The Avifauna of Laysan and the Neighbouring Islands* (1893–1900) and once again many of the original watercolours are preserved at Tring.

Keulemans confined his activities almost entirely to the pictorial depiction of birds, only writing two works himself, one of which was *A Natural History of Cage Birds* (1871). He was a serious and introspective man, who enjoyed family life; during his last years he lived quietly at Southend and died there in 1912.

Amazon Kingfisher

Chloroceryle amazona

Richard Bowdler Sharpe was only twenty-one years old when he began publication of his monograph of the kingfishers, yet he was already librarian of the Zoological Society and had earned himself sufficient respect to obtain the full cooperation of such important personages as Professor Schlegel 'who not only did his utmost to assist me during my visit to Leiden, but allowed me to bring to England all the specimens which I considered indespensible to the satisfactory completion of my book'. Schlegel, in addition to his generosity with specimens, had introduced Sharpe to his illustrator, Keulemans, and had thus seen another of his young protégés leave Leyden for London. Like many of the earlier bird books, *A Monograph of the Alcedinidae* was privately printed for the author; Sharpe took the opportunity to secure the full support of the Fellows of the Zoological Society with his tactful dedication 'To the Viscount Walden, President, and the noblemen and gentlemen composing the Council of the Zoological Society of London'.

Sharpe described the Amazon Kingfisher as the largest of the white-bellied section of the American green-backed kingfishers, and as an especially beautiful species. The species was particularly common in South America, especially Brazil, where it had first been seen and published by Prince Maximilian; the male bird in Keulemans' plate had been procured from Brazil, while the female came from Guatemala and they were both in Sharpe's own collection. The Prince described the species as inhabiting parts of the country where there were lakes, and where water plants grew: 'here it sits in an isolated branch above the water often in the thick shade of overhanging bushes and trees, and watches for its prey'. Keulemans depicted the male bird in just such a situation.

A Monograph of the Alcedinidae or family of Kingfishers, Richard Bowdler Sharpe (1868–71), plate 24

Banded Kingfisher

Lacedo pulchella

This species, which Sharpe called *Carcineutes pulchellus*, is a native of Burma, Sumatra, Java, and Malacca where it is found 'in the thickets near streams, where it seems to feed chiefly on small crabs, which it picks up off the mud'. Clearly, the specimens differed radically since Sharpe possessed a pair which had been procured near Cheribon in Java, while the birds depicted by Keulemans were in the collection of the Leyden Museum and, presumably, were among those essential specimens which Schlegel allowed Sharpe to take to London. The specimens shown here are an old male and a female. In his introduction to the monograph, while giving full praise to Keulemans, Sharpe only gave qualified approval to the colouring of the plates. He wrote that 'it would be invidious to say anything about the way in which my artist, Mr Keulemans, has performed the task alloted to him. The attention which he has bestowed upon the work merits my highest approbation; and I only regret that in some instances the effect of his beautiful drawings has been marred by the incapacity of the colourists. The department of printing and colouring the plates has been entrusted to Mr P.W.M. Trap; and though on the whole well executed, I am sorry that I cannot give unqualified praise in some instances'.

A Monograph of the Alcedinidae or family of Kingfishers, Richard Bowdler Sharpe (1868–71), plate 96

Morty Island Kingfisher

Tanysiptera galatea

Despite Dr Bowdler Sharpe's qualified praise of the colouring of the prints, the Morty Island Kingfisher makes a magnificent plate. Sharpe described the species as 'one of the most beautiful of the *Tanysiptera*', and noted that it was distinguished from others of the genus by the large white patch on its back. The monograph contains 120 plates, most of which depict dazzlingly coloured small birds, which it is easy even for the layman, to recognize as members of the kingfisher family. However, plate 92 is set apart by its sombre tones. It depicts the Sad-coloured Kingfisher, *Halcyon funebris*, a species from the island of Gilolo which had first been published and described by Prince Bonaparte.

Sharpe's frustration at the lack of control that he was able to exercise over the colouring of the plates was probably responsible, in part at least, for the fact that in later life he had his daughters trained to carry out this fine if rather unimaginative task. The three Miss Sharpes, Dora Louise, Daisy Madeline, and Sylvia Rosamund all coloured Keulemans' plates, most notably in the first edition of Sir Walter Buller's *A History of the Birds of New Zealand*.

A Monograph of the Alcedinidae or family of Kingfishers, Richard Bowdler Sharpe (1868–71), plate 101

Hairy-breasted Barbet

Lybius hirsutus

The Barbets are strongly built, brightly coloured, small birds that take their name from the tufts of feathers around their nostrils and from their rictal and chin bristles. The Hairy-breasted Barbet is a native of Gaboon and, like others of the family, lives deep in the great forests; it is not a gregarious bird, and chooses to live in pairs as in Keulemans' illustration rather than in larger groups. It is a non-migratory species and although its flight is swift, it is only able to travel over short distances. Basically, Hairy-breasted Barbets are sedentary birds and they do not need to move far in search of food. Their staple diet consists of insects, which the birds seek out on branches and in crevices in the bark of the forest trees, but do not pursue them on the wing.

The authors of this beautiful book, in addition to both being fellows of the Royal Zoological Society, were officers in the Indian Army; Charles Henry Tilson Marshall in the Bengal Staff Corps and his brother George Frederick Leycester Marshall in the Royal Bengal Engineers. As with most of the fine bird books it was printed privately and sold by subscription.

A Monograph of the Capitonidae or Scansorial Barbets, CHT & GFL Marshall (1871), plate 13

Emerald Toucanet

Aulacorhynchus prasinus

The British Museum *Catalogue of Birds* is a highly specialist publication, very
different from the other colour-plate bird books, which combined both art and
science as well as appealing to bibliophiles; this major feat of cataloguing was
stricly for professional ornithologists. *The Catalogue of Birds* contains the
maximum of scientific information packed into catalogue form, and even the
presentation of the volumes is that of small sturdy working manuals, in stark
contrast to the lavish size and style of more famous fine bird books. Volume
XIX, in which the present plate appears, is devoted to the *Picariae*, which was
the name formerly applied to a motley selection of groups placed next to the
Passeres or the sixth order of birds in the Linnaean classification. The volume
was written by PL Sclater and GE Shelley; Philip Sclater, Smit's first English
patron, wrote the section dealing with the toucans. The toucans are wholly
arboreal, and the genus had been the subject of a monograph by Gould (see
pages 82–85). They are colourful and rather grotesque birds, and are natives of
South America; the Emerald Toucanet is confined to western Ecuador.

Catalogue of Birds (British Museum, 1891), Volume XIX, plate 10

Black Bee-eater

Merops gularis

The family of the bee-eaters, with its bright and distinct colouring, is related to that of the kingfishers. The Black Bee-eater is confined to the west coast of Africa, where it is found from Sierra Leone down to Angola and, according to Dresser, used to be especially abundant in the Gold Coast – now Ghana. As the name implies, the Bee-eaters are insectivorous and catch their prey on the wing; the Black Bee-eater depicted here likes to select the highest branches of trees for its vantage point, and from there sallies forth in search of its prey.

Like most of the fine and rare bird books, Henry Dresser published this monograph himself and it appeared in parts on subscription. The present plate was published in part four, which appeared in April, 1885; the work as a whole was issued in five parts. Prior to the 1880s little had been published concerning the habits of the bee-eaters but, on the authority of Dr Reichenow, Dresser suggested that unlike its congeners this particular species nested in the hollows of tree trunks. However, the specimens depicted by Keulemans, which were in Dresser's own collection, are depicted in very anodyne surroundings devoid of specific references to habitat or peculiarities.

A Monograph of the Meropidae, Henry Eeles Dresser (1884–86), plate 28

Boobook Owl and Laughing Owl

Ninox novaeseelandiae (1), *Sceloglaux albifacies* (2)

Sir Walter Buller, the eminent New Zealand ornithologist, published the first edition of *A History of the Birds of New Zealand* during the 1870s. However, the following decade saw the discovery of a number of new species and, partly as a result of his writings, considerably increased documentation of those species already recorded. The Boobook Owl was known to Buller and his contemporaries as the New Zealand Owl or more familiarly as 'Morepork', which was the translation of its call. Buller tells of an incident during the Maori Wars when an officer newly arrived in New Zealand was inspecting his troops; the cry 'Morepork' was heard and repeated, which infuriated the officer who threatened to charge the culprit with insubordination, causing considerable merriment among the more experienced New Zealand soldiers.

Like most owls, the Boobook is a nocturnal species; during the day it retires into the darkest recesses of forests or into crevices in rocks, while around Auckland the extinct craters in the volcanic hills provide its favourite haunts. Buller records that 'on the approach of night its whole character is changed: the half closed orbits open to their full extent, the pupils expand till the yellow irides are reduced to a narrow external margin, and the lustrous orbs glow with animation, while all the movements of the bird are full of life and activity'.

The Laughing Owl, the Boobook's large companion on this plate, was one of New Zealand's rarest species even in the 1880s. Buller suggested that the scarcity might be due, in part at least, to the disappearance of a particular frugivorous rat *Kiore maore* which provided the principal ingredient of its diet and had been exterminated by the Norway Rat that had been introduced from Europe.

A History of the Birds of New Zealand, Sir Walter Buller, (2nd edition, 1888) Volume I, facing page 192

1

2

Australian Bittern

Botaurus poeciloptilus

Buller described the Australian Bittern at rest as standing with its body nearly erect, just as Keulemans depicted it. However, even at such moments, the Bittern was ready for the alert and at the slightest sound its whole aspect changed, as the description details; 'the neck is stretched to full length, and every movement betokens caution and vigilance'. Buller would have been familiar with this species from early childhood, as he had been born in New Zealand at Newark, Bay of Islands in 1838, the son of a Wesleyan missionary; as a boy he spent much time in remote country places, with considerable opportunity to develop his interest in ornithology. Buller spoke the Maori language and at one time ran a Maori newspaper; this familiarity with the native tongue enabled him to appreciate the folklore as well as understanding factual descriptions concerning the fauna of the country; it also helped him with his legal work in the Supreme Court, from which he retired in 1886. His training as an ornithologst apparently came from William Swainson, for whom he worked for a short time at the end of that naturalist's life.

The Australian Bittern depicted here had an even distribution throughout New Zealand, but was found especially by the lagoons and, in what the author described as, 'those "blind creeks", covered over with a growth of reeds and tangle, which are so numerous in all the low districts'. In the heat of the day the Australian Bittern remains quietly among the rushes, but towards evening it 'startles the ear with its four loud booming notes, slowly repeated, and resembling the distant roar of an angry bull'.

A History of the Birds of New Zealand Sir Walter Buller (2nd edition, 1888), Volume II, facing page 141

Pied Cormorant and Rough-faced Cormorant

Phalacrocorax varius (1), *Phalacrocorax carunculatus* (2)

Buller used the old-fashioned name of 'shag' to describe the Pied Cormorant. The Pied Shag he detailed as inhabiting much the same terrain as the Australian Bittern in the previous plate; but in comparison to the Bittern it was a much more destructive bird, most especially of carp, which had been introduced into the lakes near Auckland. Like other nineteenth-century ornithologists, Buller was not a conservationist and it is as straight forward reporting, free from comment, that he records that 'from time to time the Acclimatization Society prosecutes an active crusade (against the bird), but the Shags appear to be as plentiful as ever in all suitable localities'. To illustrate their voracious appetite he cites the fact that when killed the crops of the birds are often found to be crammed with fish, and on one occasion a Carp ten inches long was removed from the throat of a dead bird.

With regard to the Rough-faced Cormorant, which Buller calls the Emperor Shag, *Phalacrocorax imperialis*, much of his note is taken up with a sprightly and slightly barbed dispute with Philip Sclater of the Zoological Society in London who, in the *Report on the Birds of the Challenger Expedition* (1880), had identified the Emperor as the Rough-faced Shag. The contention was whether the crest on the bird's head indicated a separate species; Buller felt his arguments in favour of two distinct species were conclusive and stated that 'after a careful investigation of the subject, and a comparison of all the specimens within my reach I have decided to treat the Crested bird from the Chatham Islands as the true *Phalacrocorax imperialis*, and the uncrest New Zealand form as Gmelin's *P.carunculatus*'.

A History of the Birds of New Zealand, Sir Walter Buller (2nd edition, 1888) facing page 149

1 2

Song Thrush

Turdus philomelos

As with many other works on natural history of the latter part of the nineteenth century, Dr Bowdler Sharpe had a hand in the production of *A Monograph of the Turdidae*, which he edited after Seebohm's death. The two-volume treatise covers the entire thrush family. Although many people regard the Song Thrush as a quintessentially English species, it is noted in the text as being widespread not only throughout England, but also through Ireland, France, Spain, Portugal, Russia, Greece, Turkey, and right down to the Persian Gulf. A somewhat barbed sentence at the end of the note about the geographical spread of the Song Thrush states that 'The Gould Collection contains a specimen, said to have come from Foochow . . . but I find on examination that it is really an example of an English Song-Thrush, and some mistake has doubtless occurred as to the locality'.

Although Seebohm describes the Song Thrush as a skulking bird 'extremely fond of hiding under dense thickets and broad close foliage of evergreens where the branches sweep the ground', Keulemans has depicted the male and female of the species perched on an exposed branch with a blurred background suggestive of a clearing in a typically English woodland; the trees appear to be deciduous rather than evergreen. Like many other birds, the specific name of the Song Thrush has changed over the past 100 years; in this case from *Turdus musicus* to *Turdus philomelos*, which sounds even more musical.

A Monograph of the Turdidae or family of Thrushes, Henry Seebohm (Henry Sotheran & Co., 1902) Volume I, plate 40

John Guille Millais

1865–1931

John Guille Millais was born in London on 24 March 1865, the fourth son of
the successful Victorian painter John Everett Millais. The Millais family came
from Jersey in the Channel Islands. John Everett Millais first came to public
notice as one of the members of the Pre-Raphaelite Brotherhood, and later
achieved the distinction of being elected president of the Royal Academy and
the honour of a baronetcy, despite the scandal caused by his marriage to Effie,
the divorced wife of John Ruskin, the great nineteenth-century critic and
author, whose portrait he had painted. JG Millais was educated at Marlborough
and then at Trinity College, Cambridge. At Marlborough he was often in
trouble for indulging in the pursuit of birds, and his mastery with a small but
devastating pocket catapult known as a 'tweaker' became legendary. Many of
his holidays were spent in Scotland, where his father had property, and where
he became known to every fisherman and longshoreman from St Andrews to
Arbroath for his knowledge and tenacity, especially in search of rare birds; he
was to write many years later in his autobiography *Wanderings and Memories*,
'In the course of twenty five years I killed every British bird that it is possible
to obtain in our islands, beyond rare visitors, with the exception of the Curlew
Sandpiper in full breeding plumage'. When not in Scotland he would spend
school holidays in Shropshire with Reginald Cholmondeley at Condover Hall.
Cholmondeley kept a private zoo at Condover, and it was through him that
the young Millais met John Gould.

Millais' earliest published illustrations appeared in *The Graphic*, and he also
made drawings for Seebohm's *Charadriidae*, which latter paid for a trip to
western America. The spirit of travel and exploration was an integral part of
Millais's character, and after coming down from university he joined the

Seaforth Highlanders; his first book *Game Birds and Shooting Sketches* shows how he spent much of his leisure time when on leave. After resigning his commission and leaving the army he went to South Africa, and once again used his experiences to provide the material for a book *A Breath from the Veldt* (1892). Many books were to follow, both written and illustrated by himself: *British Deer and their Horns* (1895), *The Wildfowler in Scotland* (1901), *The Natural History of British Surface-feeding Ducks* (1902) – from which two of his plates are here reproduced (see pages 154 and 156) – *The Natural History of British Game Birds* (1909), and many others including one about his father. A number of these works reflected aspects of his travels in Africa, Iceland, America, and Canada. However, *Newfoundland and its Untrodden Ways* (1907) probably contained more new information than any other since, during 1906, he had mapped and explored 100 square miles of hitherto uncharted territory in central Newfoundland. The spirit that drove him and others of his ilk is described in *Wanderings and Memories* where he says that he 'resolved to ascend the Long Harbour River, practically a long series of rapids and overfalls, because Howley, the Government Surveyor, and an excellent traveller, had failed to do so, and said it was "impossible"'. This desire to find new territories lasted throughout his life, and in 1921, together with his son Raoul, also a painter, he went to the southern Sudan and mapped large areas of Bahr al Ghazal.

Millais described himself as a 'Jack of all trades', and was happy to have served as soldier and sailor, as well as acting as British vice-consul at Hammerfest in Norway during 1916. In addition to these duties he was an artist, zoologist, author, and landscape-gardener; the latter activity was mirrored in yet another literary work, *Rhododendrons and their Hybrids* (1917). Apart from the value of his work as an explorer, much of his achievement rests on the results of his studies of birds and animals at different stages of development and in different seasons. This important aspect of his work was not only recorded in the comparative studies published in his books, but was reflected in the natural history museum which he painstakingly assembled at his home, Compton's Brow, Horsham in Sussex.

Mallard

Anas platyrhynchos

Millais was a prolific writer on natural-history subjects; in the introduction to this monograph he describes simply the nature of the quest that lay behind his writings in general, and his work on British surface-feeding ducks in particular. 'About twenty years ago a rare duck and a wader, both in immature plumage, fell to my gun, and, eager to identify the species I searched every known work on British birds, hoping to gratify my curiosity, but in vain. Birds galore were to be found there, *but not my duck*, and all those pictured and described were adults – with little or no information as to their plumage at any other stage of their existence. Brooding over my disappointment, I finally resolved to find out for myself all that was to be learnt of these interesting creatures, their habits and modes of life, and every circumstance connected with their periodical change of plumage; and then I decided I would someday embody this information in a book for the benefit of other students of Natural History.'

Millais was active at a time of great innovations in the printing processes, and Longmans exploited several of them in this book; the two plates illustrated here are both reproduced from chromolithographs, which were printed by the Berlin firm of W Greve who had made their name in England through the excellent prints they had made from Thorburn's watercolours for Lord Lilford's *Coloured Figures*. The three-colour process was used for the more anatomical plates, while both line blocks and photogravure were exploited for the monochrome plates. The author was somewhat critical of the three-colour process and commented that some of the plates 'that involve the use of three colours are not absolutely correct, for the three-colour process has not yet been brought to perfection'.

As with many of the plates by his friend, Archibald Thorburn, Millais' illustrations to this book are composite groups of birds. However, his reasons for assembling the various specimens were rather different; in accordance with the principals stated in the introduction, he was intent on studying the plumage change, and for that purpose illustrated birds of the same species but at different stages of development. The three Mallards depicted here are figured at five, three, and six months.

A Natural History of British Surface-feeding Ducks (Longmans, Green & Co., 1902) plate 10

Shoveler

Spatula clypeata

As with the Mallards, the three immature male Shovelers depicted here are all at different stages of development; however, because the Shoveler also goes through a seasonal plumage change, the three specimens are shown at different times of year as well as at different ages. Millais lists the specimens as being eight months – February, fifteen months – October, and nine months – March. He explains the reasons for choosing the timing thus: 'by the middle of September we see the moult beginning, and from this date to the following February there is no surface-feeding duck whose plumage-change progresses so slowly. In its ordinary course there is little difference between September and January, but towards the end of the latter month a big flush of new feathers takes place . . .'. Although primarily concerned with the seasonal change of the surface-feeding ducks in the British Isles, Millais did not neglect to give the geographic distribution of the species he detailed, and with regard to the Shoveler he noted that it was second only to the Pintail in its range, nesting from Archangel to Algeria.

He described the swimming and feeding poses of the Shoveler as highly characteristic and said 'the head is buried low and held in such a position that everything is gathered and filtered across the tongue through the pectinated bristles of the mouth – these long natural sieves which are among the many wonders of Nature'. In a footnote he added 'all the Surface-feeding Ducks are well furnished with this wonderfully delicate mouth-bristle, and it is interesting to note that in proportion to the amount of feeding the Duck does on the actual water so these are developed – a perfect exposition of Darwinism'.

Natural History of British Surface-feeding Ducks (Longmans, Green & Co., 1902) plate 24

Henrik Grönvold

1858–1940

Grönvold was the last of the great nineteenth-century bird artists to settle in England, but unlike Wolf, Smit, and Keulemans he came by chance rather than intent. Born at Praestö in Denmark on 6 December 1858, he developed an early love of nature spending a lot of time drawing the birds and animals of his native land. While in his early twenties he went to live in Copenhagen, where he studied drawing before taking a job as an engineering draughtsman with the Danish artillery; subsequently he worked for a mill-builder.

With his interest in natural history he was not particularly happy spending his days drawing inanimate machinery, so when the opportunity arose to join the staff of the Danish Biological Research Station he seized it. There were, however, not many opportunities in Copenhagen for a natural history draughtsman and in 1892 he decided to emigrate to America, where he hoped to find more scope for his talents. However, he did not get beyond London since he was offered a job as an articulator in the British Museum preparing and mounting specimens. He only stayed in this post for three years, but went on working for the Museum in an unofficial capacity as an artist for many more. His immediate cause for resigning in 1895 was that he wished to join an expedition to the Salvage Islands being organized by William Ogilvie-Grant (1863–1924), a member of the Museum staff. Ogilvie-Grant compiled the final volumes of the *Catalogue of Birds in the British Museum* and then completed the companion work on eggs, to which Grönvold contributed many plates. Eggs only featured in a minor role in the earlier bird-books, but the publication of specialist documentary catalogues gave Grönvold the chance to exploit their beauty and demonstrate their diversity. In addition to the plates he executed for Ogilvie-Grant, he also drew eight plates of the eggs of the Great Auk for Professor Alfred Newton.

Grönvold quickly established a reputation as an artist after his arrival in England, and by the end of the century his work was appearing in the *Proceedings* and *Transactions of the Zoological Society*, as well as in *Ibis* in whose pages he followed in the tradition of Wolf and Keulemans. He also started submitting drawings to Lord Rothschild and many of these appeared in his journal *Novitates Zoologicae*, which was issued from his private natural history museum at Tring in Hertfordshire. Grönvold's first big commission was to illustrate Captain George Shelley's *Birds of Africa*; Shelley had resigned his commission in the army to devote himself to the study of natural history and his standard work, covering Africa south of the Sahara, lists over 2500 different species. Grönvold drew the fifty-seven plates, in which he concentrated particularly on those species which were new to science and consequently had not been depicted before. *The Birds of Tunisia* by Joseph Whitaker was to follow, for which he drew the nineteen plates that were then hand-coloured by Miss Dora Bowdler Sharpe, one of Dr Bowdler Sharpe's three daughters who had coloured Keulemans' plates for Buller's *The Birds of New Zealand*. *Birds of South America*, a vast work conceived by Lord Brabourne (1885–1915), which was to fill sixteen volumes and contain 400 plates, was virtually killed by the outbreak of war in 1914. The first volume was published in 1912 and the only other volume to appear came out in 1917, after Lord Brabourne's death, with notes by HK Swann; it was issued so that the plates that Grönvold had produced should not be wasted. Charles Chubb (1868–1914) of the British Museum had helped Brabourne with the descriptions for *Birds of South America*, and subsequently used the collection and notes of another South American explorer, Fred Vavasour McConnell, to put together *Birds of British Guiana* which Grönvold also illustrated. Unfortunately, Chubb died before publication of this work. Most of Grönvold's watercolours had to be worked from skins or zoo specimens and were of birds he had never seen in their natural habitats; his illustrations to Henry Eliot Howard's *The British Warblers* 1907–14 (see page 160) are the one exception and he excelled himself with these full and detailed plates. Happily, these were published just before the outbreak of war put an end to the more elaborate and expensive methods of printing which had produced all the great bird books of the nineteenth century.

If Grönvold was lucky with the timing of *The British Warbler*, he was also lucky in his association with the Australian mining millionaire Gregory Macalister Mathews (1876–1949) who had settled in England in 1902. Mathews was so wealthy that he could afford to ignore the fact that lithography had become an expensive and impracticable way of printing books, and that various forms of photographic reproduction had gradually been adopted by publishers both for technical and financial reasons. Finding that little had been published concerning Australian birds since Gould's great work of the 1840s and its supplement, and that a considerable amount of new material and knowledge had come to light in the intervening years, Mathews set to work to describe each genera and species. Mathews' *The Birds of Australia* appeared in twelve volumes between 1910–27; it was illustrated with 600 hand-coloured plates of which more than half were executed by Grönvold. Mathews followed this up with *The Birds of Norfolk and Lord Howe Islands and the Australasian South Polar Quadrant* (1928) and *A Supplement to The Birds of Norfolk and Lord Howe Islands, to which is added those Birds of New Zealand not figured by Buller*, published in 1936. Both of these books were illustrated by Grönvold and the latter work was the last book to be published containing hand-coloured lithographs, thus giving Grönvold the distinction of bringing down the final curtain on the era of the great colour-plate book. He died at Bedford in March 1940.

Aquatic Warbler

Acrocephalus paludicola

Writing in the preface to the first volume of his monograph on British warblers, Howard said 'when it first occurred to me to record certain facts which I had observed in regard to the behaviour of some of the Warblers, my intention was to include only those species whose habits and instincts I felt I could discuss with some authority as a result of systematic and prolonged study. But it soon became evident that the inclusion of a number of species which during migration, rest for a while on some of the most inhospitable parts of our shores, might be desirable, and I therefor decided that a coloured figure of these rarer species, together with a description of their plumage and a short account of their distribution, should form a part of this work'.

The distribution of the Aquatic Warbler, as given by Howard, was quite wide; he lists its breeding grounds as Andalusia, Portugal, Southern France, Silesia, Bulgaria, and Poland, while, being a migratory species, it heads south to Greece, Asia Minor, and North Africa for the winter. It is on these migrations that it occasionally gets off course and finds itself in the British Isles. Howard described it as 'an accidental visitor to Great Britain and nearly all the authentic instances of its occurrence have been in autumn. Most of the records come from Sussex, but it has been obtained in Leicestershire, Kent, Norfolk, Hampshire, and the Isle of Wight, Cornwall, and one was taken at the Bull Rock Lighthouse, County Cork'.

The coloured figures to which Howard referred to in the preface are chromolithographs, which, as with those of Millais' surface-feeding ducks, were printed by Greve of Berlin.

The British Warblers, a History with Problems of their Lives Henry Eliot Howard (RH Porter, 1907–14) Volume II, plate 27

Blue-breasted Pitta

Pitta mackloti

Grönvold was fortunate in the patronage of Gregory Macalister Mathews, a wealthy Australian, who was able to defy technological progress and to prolong the era of the hand-coloured lithograph by three or four decades; Grönvold, with his illustrations to Mathews' third work, *A Supplement to the Birds of Norfolk and Lord Howe Islands, to which is added those birds of New Zealand not figured by Buller*, published in 1936, finally concluded a century's production of great illustrated books. Audubon was a shade too early to take advantage of the development of lithography, but from the publication of Lear's work on parrots onwards all the great bird books were illustrated with lithographic prints hand-coloured by the artist or his assistants.

The collaboration between the Australian author and Danish artist, both of whom had settled in England, began with *The Birds of Australia*, the first volume of which appeared in 1910. The Blue-breasted Pitta had not been figured by Gould in his *Birds of Australia*, but it did appear in the supplement of 1869. Mathews suggested that the pittas, of which he listed three species, were introduced late into Australia; the species he listed, in addition to the Blue-breasted variety illustrated here, were the Noisy Pitta and the Rainbow Pitta, the rest of the family being African, Indian, or Asian species.

The Birds of Australia, GM Mathews (HF & G Witherby, 1910–27) Volume VIII, plate 424

Pink Robin and Flame Robin

Petroica rodinogaster (1, female; 2, male), *Petroica phoenicea* (3, female; 4 male)

Mathews described the Pink Robin – or Pink-breasted Robin as he called it – as a shy bird that loves to resort to places where it will not be disturbed. Its song he said 'is a series of low, twittered notes; which sounds prettily when heard in some gloomy recess in the forest'. Mathews' *The Birds of Australia* was a compilation of notes and information supplied to him by field observers, but he also drew upon, and acknowledged, any previously published sources, principally, of course, Gould's great pioneering work. Gould had shot the only specimen of the Pink Robin that he came across, when he found it in a deep ravine near Mount Lofty in South Australia.

The Flame-breasted Robin he described as the most gaudy member of the robin family; it breeds in Tasmania and in the highlands adjacent to south-eastern Australia. Mathews recorded that Gould took a nest of the Flame Robin in a street in Hobart town, while one of his correspondents, Mr Frank Littler, wrote that the bird was 'common about town gardens in the winter, with his mate in close attendance. It darts about in a sprightly manner, looking into all sorts of nooks and crannies in search of unwary insects'. Another correspondent, CF Belcher, said 'I know no more beautiful little picture than half a dozen cock Robins following the plough, and now and again turning towards one the blaze of their breasts against the background of black upturned sods glistening from the share'.

The Birds of Australia, GM Mathews (HF & G Witherby, 1910–27) Volume VIII, plate 438

White-winged Chough

Corcorax melanorhamphos

Not only was Mathews' updating of *The Birds of Australia* a mammoth task in itself, running as it does to twelve volumes, but Grönvold's contribution of 600 hand-coloured lithographic illustrations was also a major undertaking. The White-winged Chough, figured here, appears as the third last plate in the final volume. As was his regular practise, Mathews quoted a number of sources in relation to this Chough, including Gould whose note he described as extremely good. Gould said of the bird 'in disposition it is extremely tame, readily admitting of a very close approach, and then merely flying off to the low branch of some neighbouring tree. During flight the white markings of the wing show very conspicuously, and on alighting the bird displays many curious actions, leaping from branch to branch with surprising quickness, at the same time spreading the tail and moving it up and down in a very singular branch of some neighbouring tree. During flight the white markings of the manner; on being surprised it peeps and pries down upon the intruder down below, and generally utters a harsh, grating, disagreeable and tart note; at other times, while perched among the branches of the tree, it makes the woods ring with its peculiar, soft, low, very pleasing, but mournful pipe.' One of Mathews' correspondents called the species the 'wheat-growers' curse', and described the sight of great patches of the wheat crop ruined by the Chough: 'as soon as the wheat sprouts and the seed is soft this bird will pull up plant after plant, and as they come in flocks from ten to thirty they soon spoil an acre. I have counted seventy in one flock'.

In the preface to this final volume of *The Birds of Australia* Mathews assessed his work and said 'my aim has been to put on record such a list of the Birds of Australia as will contain ALL the information necessary to the future worker, as regards synonymy and dates of publication; while the life histories of the birds themselves have been contributed by competent field-naturalists'.

The Birds of Australia, GM Mathews (HF & G Witherby, 1910–27)
Volume XII, plate 598

Archibald Thorburn

1860–1935

From the final phase of the great illustrated bird books, the heirs and descendants of Audubon's *Birds of America*, Thorburn is undoubtedly the most popular artist, although his reputation rests as much, if not more, on water-colours painted for the picture market rather than for illustration. During the last half of the nineteenth century, artist's copyrights had been a very valuable commodity, and painters made more money out of reproductions of their work than they did out of the originals; the long drawn-out process of engraving had been the popular method for reproduction, but this gradually gave way to photography. Thorburn was one of the first to realize the importance of artist's proofs produced by these new methods, and his signed prints of snipe, woodcock, and other game-birds hung in many a billiard-room, passage, or mahogany panelled lavatory in Edwardian country houses. In many ways his preoccupation with picture-making influenced his approach to illustration, and sets his mature work apart from such of his contemporaries as Keulemans and Grönvold and links him to George Lodge (1860–1954) and CF Tunnicliffe (b.1901). Also, in a curious way, it makes for a direct comparison with the work of Alexander Wilson (see pages 26–29), although their reasons for choosing elaborate groupings of birds rather than individual species were totally different.

Thorburn, like Wilson, was a Scot. Born at Lasswade in Midlothian, near Edinburgh, on 31 May 1860, the son of the miniature painter Robert Thorburn (1818–85), he was educated at Dalkieth and in Edinburgh before being sent by his father to the newly founded St John's Wood School of Art in London. St John's Wood trained many of the late Victorian followers of the Pre-Raphaelite tradition; its Principal, AA Calderon, regarded the School as a crammer for aspirants to the Royal Academy Schools. Thorburn, however, did not follow this course, but he obviously benefited from the discipline even though he later claimed to have learned more from his father than from his teachers. Both his father and Calderon would have put great emphasis on the importance of detail. The plates from *British Birds* which are illustrated here are typical of the format he developed, in which related species are depicted gathered together rather unnaturally in some sort of generally appropriate setting. However this was not typical of his early work, which was more

obviously in the Gouldian tradition.

The first important book he illustrated was *Familiar Wild Birds* by Walter Swaysland, a Sussex naturalist and taxidermist; this work, published in four small volumes between 1883–88 dealt with all the familiar birds of the English countryside from owls to sparrows, which Thorburn illustrated with one specimen to each plate, setting them with suitable foregrounds. His accomplishment in delineating the bird and in capturing the detail and texture of its plumage immediately attracted the attention of Lord Lilford, who was in the process of publishing his major work *Coloured Figures of the Birds of the British Islands*, and was looking around for a reliable illustrator to take on the task which had been begun by Keulemans, but was now in danger of coming to a halt as his chief artist was sick. Lilford had started publishing *Coloured Figures* in 1885; Thorburn started working for him two years later and contributed over 250 plates to the seven-volume work. Lilford was an exacting task-master and knew exactly what he expected from each plate. Thorburn became a frequent visitor to Lilford, where his host kept an extensive collection of birds on his estate, which in addition to aviaries included a pinetum, falconer's quarters, and ponds; he painted a number of the most interesting and exotic residents for Lord Lilford's own collection, in addition to the British birds he drew for *Coloured Figures*. Lord Lilford died in 1896 two years before the final part of his great work was published. Unlike most of the other artists, Thorburn concentrated almost entirely on species native to the British Isles, although he did provide illustrations for LHL Irby's *The Ornithology of the Straits of Gibraltar* (1895), and to the supplement to HE Dresser's *Birds of Europe* (1895–96). He was back on his favourite ground with his contributions to the great naturalist and writer, WH Hudson, for whose *British Birds* he supplied illustrations, and also with his own books, *British Birds* (1915), *British Mammals* (1900) and *Naturalist's Sketch Book* (1900).

The tradition of ornithological books illustrated with engravings or lithographs, usually hand-coloured, just extended into the twentieth century, thanks to such wealthy amateurs as GM Mathews who were prepared to meet the financial costs of such productions. Thorburn, with his own books, was dealing with commercial publishers with the result that his watercolours were reproduced by photographic means, thus removing them from the great tradition of Audubon and Gould. A member of the British Ornithologists' Union and Fellow of the Zoological Society, Thorburn was also a keen sportsman, and it was in his depiction of game birds and wildfowl that he truly excelled. He died at Hascombe, near Godalming in Surrey, on 9 October 1935.

Wryneck, Lesser Spotted Woodpecker, Kingfisher, Green Woodpecker, Great Spotted Woodpecker and Roller

Jynx torquilla (1), *Dendrocopos minor* (2), *Alcedo atthis* (3), *Picus viridis* (4), *Dendrocopos major* (5), *Coracias garrulus* (6)

The watercolours Thorburn made to illustrate his own book on British birds are really a series of vignettes combined into a single picture, with the sole purpose of illustrating the maximum number of species in the most economical way. Although advances in technology had made production easier, the First World War, which had broken out the year before this book was published, and inflation, had made publishers and public very cost conscious. These factors combined to make *British Birds* visually less attractive than any of those already considered, although it served as a useful ready reference work for the amateur ornithologist or the mildly curious. One unattractive feature of the printed plates, not noticeable in reproduction, is that they are bled off the edge of the page leaving no margin to act as a visual frame. The great and fine bird books of the previous 200 years had all been issued in parts to subscribers; Longmans, who published Millais' *Natural History of British Surface-feeding Ducks* as well as Thorburn's *British Birds*, were catering for a new market which was being created by the rapidly expanding middle classes and the increase of leisure.

Thorburn's notes were accurate but in no way profound; they were carefully balanced to appeal to Longmans' readership. He noted the interesting fact that while the Wryneck normally lays between seven and ten eggs, if these are removed, the bird continues to lay; he then instanced a Mr Norden who had by this process induced a bird to lay forty-two eggs between 29 May and 13 July 1872. His description of the Green Woodpecker was clearly based on careful study and in his account of its method of feeding he said 'when searching for timber beetles and grubs in trees, it begins near the ground and works upwards usually in a spiral course, with short quick jumps, using its tail as a support, and inserting its tongue into the cracks and openings in the bark as it ascends, while it occasionally stops to cut away a piece of bark or decayed wood which conceals some delicacy within'.

British Birds (Longmans, Green & Co., 1915) Volume II, plate 24

Common Partridge, Red-legged Partridge and Quail

Perdix perdix (1), *Alectoris rufa* (2), *Coturnix coturnix* (3)

Thorburn was at his best illustrating game birds, and although the plates in *British Birds* cannot rival those that Wolf drew for Elliot's various monographs – especially those for the Pheasants and Grouse (see pages 116 and 122) – this plate is a far more cohesive and naturalistic treatment of the species depicted, than the composite grouping of the Wryneck, Woodpeckers, and Kingfisher that we have just considered.

Of the Common Partridge, Thorburn said that there was hardly a more popular bird in the British Isles; they are widely distributed throughout Europe from Scandinavia to the Mediterranean. According to Thorburn the Red-legged or French Partridge was introduced into England during the eighteenth century, and was first turned out in Suffolk in 1770; but other sources say that it was introduced a century earlier during the reign of Charles II. Quails on the other hand have been popular since Tudor times, and Shakespeare said of Falstaff that he was 'an excellent fellow and one who liked quails'. These little birds, which have played such an important part in the gourmet's diet since the days of the Pharoahs, are really summer visitors to England, although they have on occasions remained throughout the winter. Thorburn rendered the cry of the Quail as 'wet-my-lips'.

British Birds (Longmans, Green & Co., 1915), Volume III, plate 58

Black Guillemot, Common Guillemot, Razorbill, Great Auk, Puffin, Brünnich's Guillemot and Little Auk

Cepphus grylle (1), *Uria aalge* (2), *Alca torda* (3), *Pinguinus impennis* (4), *Fratercula arctica* (5), *Uria lomvia* (6), *Plautus alle* (7)

British Birds contains a total of eighty colour plates, but Thorburn managed to pack 400 different species into those plates. The plate of the guillemots, Razorbills, Puffins, and auks is one of the most densely crowded, depicting seven different species. The Great Auk, which Lear had figured for John Gould (see page 7), is a surprising inclusion as it had been extinct since the middle of the nineteenth century. Thorburn calls it this 'much lamented bird' and describes its destruction, which was 'ruthlessly carried out, partly in the first instance by fishermen for food and bait, and as the bird became scarcer its extermination was completed to furnish specimens and eggs for collectors and museums'. With the Black Guillemot, Thorburn depicts it in both its summer and winter plumage to show the startling change, and contrasts its brilliant red legs and feet with those of the Common Guillemot and Brünnich's Guillemot; the latter is only an occasional winter visitor to the east coast of the British Isles. Thorburn obviously enjoyed throwing in little snippets of history, as in his note on the Puffin he stated that 'in 1345, according to a document from which an extract is given in Heath's *Islands of Scilly*, these islands were held of the Crown at a yearly rent of 300 Puffins, or 6s.8d., being one-sixth of their estimated annual value.'

British Birds (Longmans, Green & Co., 1915) Volume IV, plate 76

Index